DRINKING FROM THE WELLS
OF NEW CREATION

Drinking from the Wells of
NEW CREATION

The Holy Spirit and the Imagination
in Reconciliation

Kerry Dearborn

CASCADE *Books* • Eugene, Oregon

DRINKING FROM THE WELLS OF NEW CREATION
The Holy Spirit and the Imagination in Reconciliation

Cascade Books
An Imprint of Wipf and Stock Publishers
199 W. 8th Ave., Suite 3
Eugene, OR 97401

www.wipfandstock.com

ISBN 13: 978-1-62032-627-5

Cataloging-in-Publication data:

Dearborn, Kerry

Drinking from the wells of new creation : the Holy Spirit and the imagination in reconciliation / Kerry Dearborn.

xii + 160 p. ; 23 cm. —Includes bibliographical references.

ISBN 13: 978-1-62032-627-5

1. Imagination—Religious aspects—Christianity. 2. Christian life. I. Title.

BR115 .I6 D3 2014

Manufactured in the U.S.A.

For Dr. John Perkins, whose suffering from oppression, poverty, discrimination, and racism has not robbed him of vision and love, but by Christ's love and the power of the Holy Spirit has dreamed dreams and courageously persisted in God's new creation, so that all God's children may flourish together. By the movements he has inspired and the lives he has touched, he has led countless numbers to drink from the wells of God's infinite love, and to grow as ambassadors of justice and reconciliation.

Contents

Acknowledgments

This work has developed from a life of bewilderment that though the grace of God is such a rich reservoir of love and inclusion, God's people often live parched, disconnected, and fragmenting lives. Vicarious early experiences from my mother's stories about her life in Ecuador with my father, as well as having visited and lived in numerous culturally diverse contexts, have fueled a sense of gratitude for the many ways in which our varied cultures, communities, and personalities are enriching for the world and God's kingdom. It has puzzled me that, rather than enjoying and learning from our cultural riches as the body of Christ, we have often been threatened by difference, and fostered greater divisions than unity. Even so, I have been inspired by many people, who have been freed by God to cross barriers, and who have embraced diverse others through the power of the Holy Spirit. Thank you, dear brothers and sisters in Christ, for being willing to reflect a different possibility and hope to the world. Thank you John Perkins, Willie Jennings, Emmanuel Katongole, Chris Rice, Tali Hairston, Joe Snell, Max Hunter, Doug Strong, Brenda Salter-McNeil, Sami Awad, Salim Munayer, Maggy Barankitse, and Angelina Atyan for extending God's love to me and faithfully living out the call to reconciliation by the power of God in your lives. I'm also deeply grateful for close friends who have prayed for me and encouraged me deeply in this process, the Strongs, Feldmans, Ulricksons, Broweleits, Van Duzers, Sines, and members of the Bethany Presbyterian Church community.

I want to acknowledge the assistance of many people in helping me with research issues and challenges in the writing of this book. Thank you, Steve Perisho and Cindy Strong, wise and insightful Seattle Pacific University librarians, for your ready willingness to help me at a moment's notice. Thank you, teaching assistants over the years, who have gathered data and articles for me for this project, especially Shannon Smythe, Lauren Ten Harmsel Henricksen, Christina Davis, Becca Borgh, and Michelle Ramage. Thank you dear SPU colleagues who have engaged me in rich conversations and taught me so much. I am especially grateful for Daniel Castelo and Rob Wall, and former colleague Randy Maddox (now at Duke), who perused my manuscript and offered insightful corrections. And thank you, wonderful students, who are so eager to engage authentically with God to love and serve others in the world.

Undoubtedly, the greatest assistance has come from my family, who have been patient in pilgrimage with me living the challenges of maintaining reconciled lives in the midst of life's many ups and downs. I feel deeply honored to be Tim Dearborn's wife and Alison, Andrea, and Bethany's mother. Thank you, Tim, for reading through this material numerous times, and graciously helping me to try to live the truth that God's strength is made perfect in weakness. Thank you, Alison and Greg, for introducing us to deeper experiences of the Holy Spirit in our lives and for teaching us how to listen more carefully to the voice of Jesus. Thank you, Ken and Andrea, for your encouraging support of me throughout this project, and Andrea, for carefully proofreading the entire draft manuscript and offering your masterful editing corrections to it. Thank you, Bethany, for living so profoundly the truths about which I write in this book—your courageous and creative obedience to live by the power of the Holy Spirit in your life with those who are homeless, in jail, prison, suffering from addiction and trafficking, or simply devastated by poverty, whether in Latin America, Skagit Valley, or Kolkata. Thank you, dear grandchildren, Sam, Anna, Eli, Joy, Canon, and Ailie, for renewing in me the joy of childlike trust and faith. Through you all, God has stretched my imagination of the wonders of God's gracious provision and my hope for what is yet to come.

Introduction

Why Emphasize the Holy Spirit and Imagination
for Reconciliation Studies?

Ho, everyone who thirsts, come to the waters; and you that have no money, come, buy and eat! Come, buy wine and milk without money and without price.[1]

In *Phantastes,* which C. S. Lewis credits with baptizing his imagination, George MacDonald tells the story of Anodos, who has just come of age and is about to receive his inheritance.[2] The framework with which Anodos approaches life is one of confident mastery, self-referent pragmatism, and enough curiosity to make him wonder if there is more to life than what he has experienced. Clearly a person of strong self-esteem, Anodos expresses his sense of mastery by placing things in convenient categories. When he first meets his fairy grandmother who appears to him in "tiny woman-form" wearing a Grecian dress, he patronizes her as quaint and as a trifle to be humored. When she·enlarges herself so he will take her more seriously, he approaches her from the framework of her female sensuality and beauty, as something to be grasped.

Anodos's encounter with his fairy godmother signals the beginning of a journey in which entire paradigms for him are transformed. Traveling

1. Isa 55:1.
2. Lewis, *George MacDonald,* 21.

1

through fairyland, beyond his sphere of comfort and control, takes him through a slow process of removing the veil of certainty and self-centered autonomy. He is exposed to a much larger world of wonder, terror, grace, and interdependency. Grace comes in many forms, but primarily through cleansing and refreshing waters, wise female guides, and compelling narratives. His entire journey is awash in the gentle and pervasive presence of the redeeming Spirit of love and forgiveness. C. S. Lewis writes that through reading this book he learned to love goodness and to feel the "sweet air blowing from 'the land of righteousness.'"[3]

Though unnamed and diffuse, one senses the Spirit's presence in various messengers who seek to guide Anodos through painful temptations and to heal him after repeated failures. He is often unwilling to listen and to learn, and is inattentive to what is going on inside himself or others. If he desires something, he grabs it, regardless of how this violates the other.[4] Gentle though the Presence may be, one senses also a powerful relentlessness to transform Anodos into a more whole person. His pilgrimage slowly moves him out of his solitary, self–referential ways into a new mode of existence. Growth depends profoundly on Anodos gaining an enriched imagination that connects him so deeply with others that he begins to feel their pain, and ultimately will sacrifice his life for his beloved.

Anodos provides a helpful analog of humanity, attempting to live according to the illusion of self-sufficiency or *sicut deus,* in Bonhoeffer's terms.[5] More specifically Anodos offers a typology of the ideal "man" of dominant western culture that feeds on the illusion of autonomy, control, and conquest, yet does not seem to grasp the reason for his severe relational malnourishment.[6] MacDonald's story offers a way to envision what happens when such a person is ushered into the place of God's renewal—a place that includes refreshing waters, shared homely meals, and the truth of being one small part of the immense web of God's creation. It explores the impact on one's relationship with oneself, others, and with the Divine when the Holy Spirit cleanses, reforms, and baptizes one's imagination again and again.

3. Ibid., 21–22.

4. E.g., Anodos and the girl with the globe, the statue of the marble lady, etc. MacDonald, *Phantastes*, 62, 117.

5. Bonhoeffer, *Creation and Fall*, 111–114.

6. "The cognitive revolution demonstrated that human beings emerge out of relationships. The health of a society is determined by the health of those relationships, not by the extent to which it maximized individual choice." Brooks, *Social Animal*, 320.

Phantastes provides a powerful narrative that exposes the radical changes needed to make true shalom possible. MacDonald offers an experience in which we *see* that the isolation, alienation, and dehumanization of others are not merely intellectual problems to be solved. Self-aggrandizing actions that fracture lives and communities are not merely moral failures that require forgiveness. Rather, radical transformation must happen through being steeped in grace, through the dramatic change of one's entire model of the way life is meant to be lived, and through growing in the ability to empathize with the other.[7]

Phantastes also reveals what Jungian psychologists will only identify many decades later. Anodos is haunted by a shadow that disavows grace and the dignity of the other, and that rises up continually to distort Anodos's understanding and experience of the world. It becomes obvious that shalom cannot be achieved unless shadows are acknowledged, identified, and addressed. Will and determination are not enough. MacDonald perceptively identifies the internal, shadowy resistance we have to grace and to the goodness of others, and he reveals the very long-term process necessary to bring healing, wholeness, and restoration.

Phantastes offers a narrative rational for focusing on the Holy Spirit's role in reconciliation, particularly through the vessel of the imagination. The long and arduous journey required for Anodos's transformation demonstrates the reality that living into the wholeness of God's reconciliation requires ongoing bathing, actually steeping in the presence of the Holy Spirit. And it demands an utter shift of the way one imagines the world. We will return to the issues of shadows later in the book, and the ways in which unaddressed shadows continually subvert the work of grace, but initially we will explore more carefully these other missing emphases in peace studies, and explore the reason lasting reconciliation depends on the Holy Spirit's work through the imagination.

The theme of reconciliation has become a reservoir attracting many thirsty visitors from throughout the global church in recent decades.[8] The

---

7. I have adopted the term "model" from David Brooks, who argues that a range of models is essential if one is to avoid the tendency to cling to one model and then "amputate reality to make it fit your model." He describes the ability to adopt more complex and integrative models as the "blending of neural patterns" or "the imagination." See ibid., 260, 50.

8. The author acknowledges the contested nature of the term "reconciliation" (see De Gruchy, *Reconciliation*, 10–43). Its use in this book will be derived from its biblical and theological roots. Though reconciliation has been "*en vogue*" in many contexts outside of

rising heat of global competition for limited resources, along with national, ethnic, and racial tensions, has created extensive areas of relational drought and fearful mistrust. Thus people have come to the waters to discern the possibilities in God's invitation,

> Ho, everyone who thirsts, come to the waters; and you that have no money, come, buy and eat! Come, buy wine and milk without money and without price. . . . For as the rain and the snow come down from heaven, and do not return there until they have watered the earth, making it bring forth and sprout, giving seed to the sower and bread to the eater, so shall my word be that goes out from my mouth; it shall not return to me empty, but it shall accomplish that which I purpose, and succeed in the thing for which I sent it. For you shall go out in joy, and be led back in peace; the mountains and the hills before you shall burst into song, and all the trees of the field shall clap their hands. (Isa 55:1, 10–12)

Some visitors have waded in deeply, and have gained a sense of the costly nature of reconciliation, along with its immense gifts of renewal and refreshment. Others have visited only briefly, attempting to use its resources to advance their own political or social agenda. Debates about the meaning, source, and, process of reconciliation pervade the global church today, but at times sadly obscure God's gracious invitation and provision rather than compellingly convey it.

Much clarity has come through theologians like Karl Barth, James Torrance, Jürgen Moltmann, Miroslav Volf, Leonardo Boff, Catherine LaCugna, and Greg Jones, who have affirmed God's work of reconciliation as central to the gospel of Jesus Christ. Church leaders, including Archbishop Desmond Tutu, John Perkins, Brenda Salter-McNeil, Chris Rice, and Emmanuel Katongole, have called on the church to participate with Christ in this central work of grace. Sociologists like Curtiss DeYoung and John Paul Lederach have described the wretched consequences of living as if reconciliation is an optional extra for Christians, and have cataloged both obstacles to reconciliation and ways to move forward in sharing in the costly privilege of God's work of reconciling genders, ethnicities, and classes.

Peace and justice programs, and centers for reconciliation, have sprung up on university and seminary campuses throughout the world. Never have

---

the church and Christian theology, it is beyond the scope of this book to extensively engage the various meanings and attributions that have been offered in these other contexts to "reconciliation". See Schwöbel, "Reconciliation," 14.

people been more aware of the deep relational fractures around the world, and the immense cost of dignity, suffering, and lives where individuals or groups seek ascendency over rather than community with their neighbors. Thus, there is an expanding bibliography of articles, books, and chapters on reconciliation, which seek both to define reconciliation and describe ways it can be achieved.[9]

There are also texts that examine ways in which Christian faith has been used to defend divisions, hatred, and slavery.[10] These texts highlight the obvious fact that churches have not lived up to their calling to engage as ambassadors of reconciliation. "While there were a few very exceptions, whites in the colonial and antebellum periods generally used the experience of joint worship not to dissolve worldly hierarchies but to explain and sanctify them."[11] Similarly in the mid-twentieth century, Martin Luther King Jr. stated, "We must face the sad fact that at 11 o'clock on Sunday morning when we stand to sing 'In Christ there is no East or West,' we stand in the most segregated hour of America."[12] More recently, Christian Smith and Michael Emerson have documented the ways in which white evangelicals in America continue to be entrenched in racially segregated churches and relationships.[13]

God's people have been given many resources to share in the work of reconciliation and draw people to its healing waters, but often these resources have been resisted, even as Jonah resisted his call to reach out to the people of Nineveh. In particular, many Christians have resisted or overlooked the gift of living water in the Holy Spirit's presence to apply the reconciling work of Christ to our parched lives and communities.[14] Often there has been neglect of Jesus' fulfillment of Isaiah's invitation, "Let anyone who is thirsty come to me, and let the one who believes in me drink. As the scripture has said, 'Out of the believer's heart shall flow rivers of living water.' Now he said this about the Spirit, which believers in him were to receive . . ." (John 7:37–39a).

9. Many of these texts are included in the bibliography.

10. See, for example, Irons, *The Origins of Proslavery Christianity.*

11. Irons, http://www.spu.edu/depts/perkins/about/perspective/2009-autumn/Books Proslavery-Christianity.asp.

12. King Jr., "Can a Christian Be a Communist?"

13. Emerson and Smith, *Divided by Faith.*

14. See for example, Emerson and Smith, *Divided by Faith*; Sider, *The Scandal of the Evangelical Conscience*; and Rah, *The Next Evangelicalism.*

Reconciliation, biblically and theologically defined, has been approached largely as framed by the work of God in Christ on the cross. As Paul writes, "in Christ God was reconciling the world to himself" (2 Cor 5:19). While affirming the centrality of God's work in Christ for understanding and experiencing reconciliation, this book focuses on the work of the Holy Spirit to teach and transform believers to share with Christ in this ministry. Jesus said, "But the Advocate, the Holy Spirit, whom the Father will send in my name, will teach you everything, and remind you of all that I have said to you" (John 14:26).

In particular, this book explores one key aspect of the work of the Holy Spirit in equipping people for reconciliation, and that is in the transformation of the imagination.[15] Often, as Lederach has described, barriers to reconciliation exist where moral imagination is lacking. Bridges that overcome such barriers are found more often in transformed human hearts and vision than in cognitive theories or techniques.[16] "Understanding and deep insight [for peace building] are achieved through aesthetics and ways of knowing that see the whole rather than the parts, a capacity and pathway that rely on intuition more than cognition."[17] The Holy Spirit's work in re-creation, pouring out new visions and dreams on young and old, prophetic insights and gifts for both male and female (Acts 2:17), connects deeply with the imagination. In fact, George MacDonald wrote that a wise imagination *is* the "presence of the Spirit of God."[18]

In order to lay an appropriate foundation on which to explore the Holy Spirit's transformation of the imagination toward participation in God's work of reconciliation, this book first explores the three "moments" of salvation offered by the triune God, as conveyed by Karl Barth.[19] Though

15. It is vital to distinguish "imagination" from "imaginary" and fanciful. "Imagination" in this book will be used to refer to that center of human creativity, intuition, and vision, which offers an interpretive framework through which the world is perceived and approached. For further reading see Dearborn, *Baptized Imagination,* and Jennings, *Christian Imagination.*

16. Daniel Groody describes the impact of hearts that are opened by God's presence: "No longer judging people by external appearances, they are able to see deeper into the heart of other people, as if to begin to behold others as God does (1 Sam 16:7), as if to see the glory that resides within each and every person." Groody, *Globalization, Spirituality, and Justice,* 243.

17. Lederach, *Moral Imagination,* 69.

18. MacDonald, "Imagination," 28.

19. Three moments of salvation was the way in which James Torrance described Barth's Trinitarian framing of soteriology. He describes the three moments in *Worship,*

salvation and reconciliation are distinguishable, they are also interrelated in that salvation includes union with God and with others, and it is deeply rooted in the Hebrew idea of shalom. [20]

In the first chapter, reconciliation is affirmed as a gift of God, Father, Son, and Spirit before it is ever something in which we are called and equipped to participate. Questions such as the scope and nature of reconciliation will be addressed.

The second chapter explores the nature of the Holy Spirit and the Spirit's invitation to and application of God's gift of reconciliation in Christ to our lives. As Christoph Schwöbel writes, "The plausibility of the notions of reconciliation and peace with God depends on explicating this largely implicit pneumatological element of the model of reconciliation."[21] After briefly surveying the nature of the Holy Spirit, corollary implications for the shape of reconciliation will be explored. What does it mean to honor the Holy Spirit as God and to live responsively to the Spirit's work of new creation and new communion?

The third chapter deals specifically with the gifts of the Holy Spirit of re-creation, hope, and love. As with the first creation, the recreating work of the Holy Spirit includes the separation of light from darkness, except now that which is life-giving is cut free from that which is destructive. Jesus promised that the Spirit would come and lead us into all truth. He encouraged his followers on the eve of his death that another Advocate would be with them revealing to them everything he had taught them. They need not live in fear, but rather can receive God's love and hope for them, be freed through confession and repentance, and move forward in radical communion even in the midst of great turmoil and tribulation.

The fourth chapter focuses specifically on the work of the imagination as a vessel into which the Holy Spirit pours new life to dissolve away false notions, recreate new visions, and catalyze transformed lives. As the truth of the Spirit reaches the heart through the imagination, the believer is empowered to deny herself, take up her cross, and follow Jesus. The Holy

---

Community and the Triune God of Grace, and concludes, "There are three moments but only one act of salvation, just as we believe there are three persons in the Trinity, but only one God." Torrance, *Worship*, 76.

20. "I am positing reconciliation as both the *telos* of creation, including, therefore, rational and non-rational aspects of being, and as the process of salvation." Clegg, "Between Embrace and Exclusion," 128.

21. Schwöbel, "Reconciliation," 25.

Spirit's transformation of Peter in Acts 10 is discussed to provide instructive grounding for these ideas.

Chapter five explores the Holy Spirit's use of the imagination as both a bridge and a lofty vista. The imagination is a useful bridge with its bi-focal capacity to hold together numerous tensions without which the ministry of reconciliation can become irrelevant, exploitive, or escapist. As a lofty vista, the imagination can be used by the Holy Spirit to facilitate a larger perspective on life, on Scripture, and on the other, and to be a vehicle for seeing the kingdom of God in our midst. God's transforming influence through the Spirit's work on Paul's imagination is used to illustrate this.

Chapter six explores the challenges to reconciliation that arise from shadows within the realm of the unconscious and the imagination. Narratives by George MacDonald offer helpful ways to explore these shadows and to clarify that reconciliation is an ongoing process that requires vigilance, ongoing openness to the Holy Spirit, and specific skills of the imagination to address the distorting shadows that will arise. Deep-seated fears and self-aggrandizing pride do not die easily, but unless they are addressed by the Holy Spirit in the realm of the imagination, little progress can be made toward the relational healing that Christ's kingdom brings.

Chapter seven will conclude with three signposts that reflect the work of the Holy Spirit through the imagination and that point to oases of God's kingdom in our midst. A brief historical survey is offered of four periods of the church when the presence of the Holy Spirit was more wholeheartedly welcomed, obeyed, and allowed to guide the community of faith than at other times in history. These movements express greater openness to imaginative renewal (new moral imaginations) and in response a more profound expression of communities of reconciliation across racial, gender, class, and ethnic differences.

It is my prayer that this book can be a vehicle of the Holy Spirit to bring renewal, hope, and new openness to the work that God would do in our own contexts, that we might more effectively reflect the shalom for which we were created, and exalt our gracious God who extends loving communion to all.

1

The Reconciling God

[Reconciliation is God's gift,] "because we cannot, on our own, become reconciled to God. It is the divine sacrifice of Jesus Christ on the cross that made reconciliation possible."[1]

Radical Atonement

Much of the focus of studies and teaching on reconciliation, especially for Protestants, has been on the cross of Jesus Christ and the individual's restored relationship with God.[2] It is his sacrificial death that cleanses us from sin and creates the way for a new relationship with God the Father. Acknowledging the centrality of Jesus as the good news of who God is and what God has done is a vital emphasis. Both Barth and Bonhoeffer endeavored to correct theology that was losing this center and becoming more anthropocentric than theocentric. They discovered that a message focused more on human experience of God than the God of human experience can become dangerously manipulated for hu-

1. Nalunnakkal, "Come Holy Spirit," 14.

2. See Baum, "A Theological Afterward," 184–92, for contrasts between more private and individualistic interpretations of reconciliation and the more social approach of Roman Catholics. See also Wan, *Power in Weakness,* 87, in which biblical exposition reveals that *new creation* is a communal not an individualistic term.

man ends, rather than leading to transformation into Christlikeness.[3] Barth and Bonhoeffer worked to reclaim the centrality of Christ's life, death, and resurrection for the church and its participation in God's purposes for the world.

This Christ-centered emphasis correlates with the emphasis of much Christian theology throughout the ages. Paul stated, "I longed to know nothing but Jesus Christ and him crucified" (1 Cor 2:2).[4] Luther stated, "true theology and recognition of God are in the crucified Christ. The cross of Christ is the only instruction in the Word of God there is, the purest theology."[5] Eberhard Jüngel wrote that "the basic aporia into which European theology has blundered" under the dictatorship of metaphysics is to "think of God without thinking of him simultaneously as the Crucified."[6] Miroslav Volf more recently affirmed Paul's central focus on the cross as the basis from which Volf's reflections on "exclusion and embrace" derive.[7]

However, there have been times in which certain views of the cross and certain Christ-centered emphases have been used to obscure the biblical focus on salvation as reconciliation with God and with others, and to marginalize the Holy Spirit in particular. As central and wondrous as the cross is to healing and restoring our relationship with God, problems arise when the cross is seen exclusively through the interpretive lens of penal substitution.[8] Such framing of God's work of salvation can both inhibit our willingness to trust a Father who demands such sacrifice and eclipse the union with God that Jesus' *life*, death, *and resurrection* create. In other words, it can obscure the ontological reality that we are saved in and through our having become united with God in Jesus Christ.[9]

3. Though contextual theologians have rightfully challenged as a modernist fallacy the false dichotomy between an emphasis on our subjective experience of God and one on a supposedly objective view of the God of our experience, this author intends to honor the appropriate ways in which Bonhoeffer and Barth shifted the emphasis in their theology from anthropological preoccupations to a more central Trinitarian reference point.

4. Cf. Volf, *Exclusion and Embrace*, 25.

5. Luther, *Operationes in Psalmos*, 34. See also Luther, *Heidelberg Disputation*, 1518.

6. Jüngel, *God as Mystery of the World*, 39. "The cross of Jesus Christ is the ground and measure of the formation of metaphors which are appropriate to God." Jüngel, *Theological Essays*, 65.

7. Volf, *Exclusion and Embrace*, 25.

8. Schwöbel writes, "It is interesting to note that the model of reconciliation we see developed [in Romans 5:1–11] is wider than any notion of sacrificial death or penal substitution." "Reconciliation," 19.

9. Cf. Barth: "Sound theology can only be 'unionistic,' uniting God and man." "A

Rather, atonement begins in Jesus' birth, when he comes to be one with us and to share fully in our frail humanity. Jesus is tempted in every way as we are, yet offers a perfect response of obedience on our behalf and in our place. Reconciliation is not merely the paying of a debt but the healing and re-creation of defiled humanity through Jesus' uniting his life with ours, and turning our fleeing humanity, through his love and obedience, back toward the welcoming arms of the Father. Because our oneness with Christ begins with his birth and life,[10] Paul clarifies that we share in his baptism and in his death.[11] "We have been crucified with Christ, it is no longer we who live but Christ, and the life we now live, we live by the faith of him who loved us and gave his life for us" (Gal 2:20).

If we are going to let reconciliation bear its real fruit in our lives, we must accept that these are no longer our lives, that we have died, and the life we live is Christ's alone. Thus, Christians are not merely justified by grace, but transformed by grace, for we have been put to death by grace and given a new life and identity.[12] Even so, the Holy Spirit is to be honored as the one who indwells God's people and enlivens us to live as those who have been re-created in Christ and are in the process of being recreated daily. As Christoph Schwöbel writes, "The Spirit is the transforming power that allows believers to participate in Christ's way from death to life and so establishes, on the basis of the reconciliation achieved in Christ, a relationship to the love of God in Christ that cannot be broken by any power, not even by the most powerful cosmic forces."[13]

Theological Dialogue," 172

10. "Christ's Incarnation is already an act of salvation." Ware, *Orthodox Way,* 78. See also Calvin: "In short, from the time when he took on the form of a servant, he began to pay the price of liberation in order to redeem us." *Institutes,* Vol. 1, Book II, Chapter XVI, Section 5, 507.

11. Gal 3:27: "And all who have been united with Christ in baptism . . ."; Rom 6:4; Gal 2:20.

12. Cf. Kathleen Hughes, who notes how our celebration of the Eucharist reflects such transformation: "Participation in the liturgy means participation in the life, death and rising of Jesus, *truly* dying and rising with him, *truly* laying down our lives. Participation means working mightily for the establishment of the reign of God by letting the spirit of God work in us to complete Christ's work on earth." "Liturgy and Justice," 50–51.

13. Schwöbel, "Reconciliation," 20.

Three Moments of Salvation

Creation in God's Image

Because Karl Barth took so seriously the revelation of God in Jesus Christ, he understood salvation as being composed of three great moments of God's work among us. Jesus points continually to the Father and the Father's great love. Salvation, seen as communion with God, begins when God from all eternity chooses to create us as part of God's own people.[14] Creation instantiates the first moment of salvation, with grace, freedom, and intimate relationship for humans with God.[15] Human identity is stamped with God's own regal image, with the gift of participation in God's gracious rule and creativity. As Rikk Watts writes, "the biblical language indicates that all human beings—not just the Pharaohs of Egypt—in their physicality, their maleness and femaleness, and their interplay between individual and collective, are intended to be living pictographs of Yahweh the Creator, enlivened by his breath . . . and ultimately by his indwelling Spirit."[16] Shalom with God, with others, and with all creation offers a hopeful image of God's saving intentions in this first moment of creation.

Wonderful Exchange in Christ

Barth describes Jesus' life, death, and resurrection as the second aspect of salvation since God's original gift of shalom was shattered by humans who refused grace. "And this is our rebellion: the fact that we want everything, all that is noble, helpful and good . . . but not this thing, namely, to allow ourselves to be made open, prepared and made fit for God by God. *Grace* is God's sovereign realm. But our enmity toward God . . . the evil that we do; this precisely is our *hostility* toward *Grace.* . . . We cannot abide deity."[17]

14. "God in this Jesus has loved us—truly all of us—from eternity, because God has chosen to be our loving Father and had chosen us all to become his beloved children in order to save us all and draw us to himself" Barth, "Teach us to Consider," 165. "Creation is . . . the area and ground of God's great final work of redemption" Barth, "Theological Dialogue," 172.

15. This is not in any way to diminish the wonder of God's creation of the nonhuman world and to place humans over and against the natural world. That is just not the focus of this book at this point.

16. Watts, "New Exodus/New Creational Restoration of the Image of God," 21.

17. Barth, *The Holy Spirit and the Christian Life,* 19–20.

As Bonhoeffer writes, we have claimed a false identity of "*sicut deus*" rather than "*imago Dei.*"[18]

Not content to trust God and God's ways, humans have asserted their own self-defined identity and the pretense that they could be "like God" making their own judgments as "authors" of their own lives. J. R. R. Tolkien offers a powerful depiction of such hubris in *The Silmarillion* with Melkor, who is not content to draw his life and creativity from the flame of the One, Iluvatar. He withdraws to the barren places to seek his own autonomous source of life and creativity, and thus provokes dissonance and distortion. As with human history, dominance and oppression become Melkor's ways, rather than loving resonance with God's gracious creativity.[19]

God's intentions of shalom for humankind remain, however, and it is with a view to extend salvation to every family in every nation on earth that God forms a covenant people. It is through this community that light will extend to all the nations.[20] Their identity is again stamped with a regal image, as the beloved of God (Isa 43), and they are given a covenant purpose to be God's people through whom the nations might glimpse the wonder of God's saving love and be drawn toward this light. They are the one on behalf of the many.[21]

Even so they prefer to live on behalf of themselves, rejecting God's gift of gracious election, with each one doing what is right in his or her own eyes. Still, a story of covenant faithfulness emerges where God's long-suffering love endures generation after generation of rebellious children, with God repeatedly offering all that is needed for shalom. The vine of Israel, planted to grow in response to God's love for them and to bear fruit for the nations, has to be pruned, divided, and transplanted continually until only a stump remains.[22] And it is out of this stump that God raises the True Vine, Jesus Christ, Savior and Messiah.

---

18. See Bonhoeffer, *Creation and Fall*, 111–14.

19. Tolkien, *Silmarillion*, 3–12.

20. Cf. Wright, on God speaking to Abraham, "through you all the nations on earth will find blessing": "The vision is universal. . . . So Abraham is actually a fresh start for the world. This promise is God's great manifesto. This text is God's declaration of his mission, which is nothing less than the blessing of all nations." *Knowing the Holy Spirit*, 98. "Israel in the Old Testament was not chosen *over against* the rest of the nations, but *for the sake of* the rest of the nations." Wright, *Knowing the Holy Spirit*, 100.

21. For more on the concept of "the one and the many" see Torrance, *Worship*, 47–52, and Volf, *Exclusion and Embrace*, 47–51.

22. See Isaiah 11:1–9.

Thus for Barth the second movement of God's salvation is in Jesus' life, death, and resurrection. God comes in Christ to fulfill the covenant and become more than a mere example of true humanity. Christ becomes the very fount from which our new life springs. Christ doesn't merely show the way, but he is the way, offering his own life for the transformation and ongoing sustenance of all people. "This union between God and man has not been made only in Jesus Christ but in him as our representative for the benefit of all men [sic]."[23] Christ takes on himself the burdens that enslave, divide, and oppress, and offers a "wonderful exchange" of the peace of living from a new center in God.[24] His teaching and his life also cleanse the foul and hopeless images of life by which we have been cowed and subdued. T. F. Torrance describes the incarnation as Jesus Christ receiving the Holy Spirit "with all of his consuming holiness into the human nature which he took from our fallen and alienated condition."[25] As Walter Wangerin depicts in "The Ragman," this is a glorious exchange indeed, for he takes our bleeding wounds, our bitter personalities, our hopeless alienation into himself, and offers instead participation together in the very life of God.[26]

One can see a contemporary analogy of this wonderful exchange and its impact in the film *The Green Mile*. John Coffey (J. C.) is unjustly convicted and on death row waiting for execution, yet is smuggled out by the prison wardens in the dead of night because of his gift of healing.[27] They drive him to the home of the chief warden, where the warden's wife lies dying from a brain tumor. Her beauty has been ravaged by the tumor, and her Southern charm distorted, so foul epithets hurl forth from her mouth. She has been cut off from hope, from mutuality in relationships and from wholeness. J. C. is able to see the tumor and to offer her the kiss of life in

23. Barth, "A Theological Dialogue," 172.

24. James Torrance, *Worship*, 15, 46, 89, 90. "The Greek word *katallassein* means quite literally 'to effect and exchange,' . . . So it comes to mean 'to reconcile,' to exchange friendship for enmity, love for hatred, peace for hostility." Torrance, *Worship*, 90.

25. T. F. Torrance, *Theology in Reconstruction*, 247.

26. Wangerin, "The Ragman," 3–6.

27. *The Green Mile*, directed by Darabont, 1999, DVD. Similar to Greg Jones's practice in *Embodying Forgiveness*, I also include in this book references to narrative, literary, and film works "not in order to make points accessible to nontheological audiences. . . . My references to these works are integral elements of my theological arguments" Jones, *Embodying Forgiveness*, xv. In addition, the very nature of this book, on the power of the Holy Spirit to work through the imagination, invites the use of imaginative ways of conveying ideas.

which he sucks out of her mouth all that is killing and defiling her, and absorbs it into his own being.

This healing encounter offers a powerful depiction of Ephesians 2:14 and Galatians 3:28 where Paul describes Jesus Christ's destruction of dividing walls and reconstitution of us as united in Christ across ethnic, socio-economic, and gender barriers. A white Southern privileged woman being kissed and healed by a black, incarcerated man on death row evokes the wonder of Jesus' gift of healing through his life and death. In Jesus' willingness to submit to false accusation, incarceration, and the death penalty he swallowed up death forever and created one new humanity in which there is "neither Jew nor Gentile, slave nor free, male and female" (Gal 3:28).[28] Whereas John Coffey sucked out and swallowed the disease of the warden's wife to fully restore her, Jesus, Son of God and Son of Man, is able to absorb the sins of the world and offer cleansing and re-creation to reunite us with God and with others.

As Peter Kuzmic clarified when preaching on Ephesians 2 in the midst of bombing raids on his city during the Balkan conflict, "Christ the Reconciler [has] 'made the two one' by destroying the enmity. . . . God does not kill the enemy, but the enmity. . . . The enemies are candidates for salvation. They are loved by God."[29] He went on to explain that the cross of Christ makes all the difference. We worship a God "who would not shed the blood of his enemies, but would in his divine redemptive plan allow the blood of his righteous son to be shed so that we, enemies of Him and of each other, may be forgiven and reconciled."[30]

Barth describes the reconciling exchange wrought by the Father and the Son: "What happened [in the death of Jesus] was not an act of God's enmity against man. No, on the contrary, because God in this Jesus has loved us—truly all of us—from eternity, because God has chosen to be our loving Father and has chosen us all to become his beloved children in order to save us all and draw us to himself, for that purpose, he has in Jesus written off, rejected, crucified, slain, not *us* but our old man, however mightily he may live and clamor in us. Precisely for our sake, so that we ourselves may live as free men [sic], he has in the death of Jesus removed the old man in *us*, washed him away, consumed him in fire, smoke, and ashes."[31] Similarly,

28. Similarly, Isaiah prophesied that the Lord of Hosts "will swallow up death forever" (Isa 25:7).

29. Kuzmic, ""Reconciliation in Eastern Europe," 53.

30. Ibid.

31. Barth, "Teach us to Consider," 165.

Father Greg Boyle writes, God's love "doesn't melt who you are, but who you are not."[32]

Outpouring of the Spirit

The third moment of salvation for Barth is the outpouring of the Holy Spirit into those who share in Christ's death and new life. "[God] teaches us in the complete fire of his Holy Spirit to consider that we must die, that Jesus has died for us. My dear brothers and sisters, if only a spark of this fire should fall into the heart of a man, then—however he be—for this man nothing is lost, everything is won."[33] Jesus promised to come with the Father and dwell in his people by the Holy Spirit. Our baptism means both dying with Jesus and rising with him that we may be filled with his Spirit, and thus new life, new identity, and new visions of life. Baptism is a profound identification with Jesus' death and resurrection, calling for radical transformation from living by one's own inclinations to living in Christ by the power of the Holy Spirit. Eucharist is an ongoing recommitment to join with Jesus in his dying and rising, and to live by his Word and Spirit, rather than the seductive nourishment of lesser identities.

Aversion to death in Christ is often where Christians remain stunted in growth and thwarted in reconciliation. Letting go of lesser identities and refusing to feed the hungry monster of the old self[34] is difficult in contexts where self-actualization, self-fulfillment, and self-realization form the trinity of exalted achievement.[35] A close relative's recent death was a reminder of just how difficult it is for us to "die." Though a lifelong Christian and a giving person, her highest value was independence. Thus, loss of power and control were utterly repugnant to her. But her last few weeks of life ushered in complete vulnerability, relinquishment of almost all possessions, and

32. Boyle, *Tattoos on the Heart*, 103.

33. Barth, "Teach us to Consider," 166. There are significant debates about Barth's pneumatology, whether he does justice to the personhood of the Holy Spirit, and whether he is Catholic and/or evangelical in his views of the Spirit's work. For a helpful summary see Buckley, "A Field of Living Fire: Karl Barth on the Spirit and the Church," 81–102. It is beyond the scope of this book to enter into this debate. That God works through the Holy Spirit to enliven people with the life of Christ and draw them into God's reconciling grace is this book's operating claim and is consistent with Barth's own pneumatology.

34. See Bantum, "Why Christians Can't Be Post-Racial."

35. David Brooks describes American culture as having moved from a "culture of self-effacement to self-expression." Brooks, "The Humility Code."

utter feebleness. She could accomplish nothing and had to put her trust totally in God's love for her in Christ. Her moment of greatest freedom and peace came just two days before she died, when she could finally let go and pray, "Thy will be done."

The process of my relative's dying provides a radical vision of what it means to die into Christ and to live by the power of the Holy Spirit. It requires complete relinquishment of the illusions of autonomy and independence. This should not surprise those who would be one with Jesus, for Jesus exemplified this in every way. "I can do nothing on my own . . . ," he humbly acknowledged. "I do only what the Father does" (John 5:30). He lived his life in utter dependence on the Father and for the glory of the Father by the power of the Spirit.[36] Complete vulnerability and Spirit-filled dependency marked his life from his homeless birth to his degrading death.

Furthermore, Jesus says to those who would be his disciples, "Take up your cross daily and follow me" (Luke 9:23). Vision, power, and life in the Spirit remain stunted because we so often prefer to live by the dictates of our old identities rather than from a crucified self and new life in Christ. The Holy Spirit comes to empower God's people to say, "Thy will be done," to cleanse the scales from our eyes that blind us to God's vision of reconciliation, and to free us in vulnerability to become the beloved community— God's new creation in Christ. Perhaps resistance to this comes because we have yet to discover what John Perkins learned, that "to deny yourself is not to abandon yourself but to throw yourself into the loving arms of God."[37] Perhaps God's invitation to new life in the Spirit has been muted because many Christians have ignored the wonder of God as triune. Perhaps it is because the central tangible reminders of the drama of death and new life in the Spirit have become so reduced in meaning.[38]

Baptism and communion in numerous churches have been relegated to the margins of church life, seldom celebrated and then only as a brief and seemingly extraneous part of the service. Rather than being nourished on

36. Jesus was conceived by the Spirit, anointed by the Spirit in baptism, driven out into the wilderness by the Spirit, prayed in the Spirit, and was raised from the dead by God's Spirit. Cf. Moltmann: "*Christ's history in the Spirit* begins with his baptism and ends in his resurrection." *Source of Life*, 15.

37. Perkins, "Contexts of the Journey of Reconciliation." Cf. Jones: "This does not involve . . . the 'death' of selves through annihilation. Rather it is learning to see one's self and one's life in the contexts of communion." *Embodying Forgiveness*, 6.

38. "The gospel is thus a truth widely held, but a truth greatly reduced." Brueggemann, *Finally Comes the Poet*, 1.

life in the Spirit that flows from dying and rising with Christ, some Christians have often focused almost exclusively on "justification by faith." As Gordon Fee writes, "Any careful reading of Paul's letters makes it abundantly clear that the Spirit is the key element, the *sine qua non*, of all Christian life and experience. To put that in theological perspective, it needs to be noted that, contrary to historic Protestantism, 'justification by faith' is not the central theme of Pauline theology."[39] And whereas the early church practiced communion regularly as a joyous reminder of Christ's death and resurrection and believers' participation by the Spirit in his dying and rising (Rom 8:11), communion in many denominations has come to be an irregular and somber event focused primarily on forgiveness of sin.

God offers us nourishment for life through both Word and Spirit and comes to meet with us at the Lord's Supper. It was at his last supper with his disciples that Jesus pledged his peace to them and reminded them of their true identity, as branches of the true vine. In his vulnerable hours before crucifixion, he reminded them that they too were utterly dependent, that "apart from me you can do nothing" (John 15). They were not servants but friends, into whom Jesus would pour his Spirit that he might be present with them always and lead them in his way. Thus, this third moment of salvation, power to live out restored shalom with God and God's people, is rooted in and constantly nourished by *communion* experienced at the table.[40]

Brueggemann identifies three ways in which the Spirit nourishes God's people to live into the vision of God's reconciliation by God's power. First, "At the table we drink to another reality and toward another order."[41] Here the Spirit renews a vision of what it means to follow Christ and to be released from our own petty identities and agendas.[42] Here we celebrate the kingdom of God in our midst and deepen our imaginative capacity to perceive God's realm.

39. Fee, *Listening to the Spirit in the Text*, 37.

40. The obvious irony remains that this is such a contentious and divided place for Christians. Barth asserted: "Now we shall have to win and assert freedom for our one Lord Jesus Christ in spite of these divided Lord's Suppers." "No Christian Marshall Plan," 1331.

41. Brueggemann, *Living Toward a Vision*, 143.

42. Cf. Cavanaugh: "To participate in the Eucharist is to live inside God's imagination. It is to be caught up into what is really real, the body of Christ. As human persons, body and soul, are incorporated into the performance of Christ's *corpus verum*, they resist the state's ability to define what is real." *Torture and Eucharist*, 224–25.

Second, at the table, the Spirit reminds us that "true life is in mystery and not in management."[43] Jesus is the host and center of all that happens at the table. We join with others as welcome guests who relinquish control and receive the wonder of communion with God and with those very unlike ourselves.

Third, at the table, it becomes clear that "we are the Lord's and not ours."[44] Our lives belong to God and have become earthen vessels for the treasure that God would pour out for the world. Brueggemann warns that it is all too easy to betray the mystery of the table and to try to take the ministry of reconciliation into our own hands as a task we must accomplish: "we doom our *shaloming* to failure, either in pride or despair, before we even begin."[45] He continues, "But it does begin at the table. It always does. And the promise to us is that the church that lets this historical mystery fashion its life can hear the word and can be empowered to live in and toward the new age of *shalom*."[46]

Reconciliation will never be our achievement, but is God's symphonic gift to us through three movements of creation, redemption, and renewal. Thus, "*reconciliation is more a question of spirituality than a strategy*."[47] This accords with the crux of our argument that if we neglect the present work of God through the Holy Spirit in reconciliation, we enfeeble our efforts, reducing them to a human-centered activity rather than participation in God's great work. The invitation is to drink from the wells of new creation through reliance on the Holy Spirit who empowers us to share in the joyous comm-unity of the triune God.

43. Brueggeman, *Living Toward a Vision*, 143.

44. Ibid.

45. Ibid., 144.

46. Ibid.

47. Kuzmic, "Reconciliation in Eastern Europe," 54. Cf. Schreiter, *Ministry of Reconciliation*, 16.

2

Who Is the Holy Spirit and
How Does the Spirit Effect Reconciliation?

If our worship and witness are conspicuous for their lack of Holy Spirit, it is
surely because we Protestants, whatever we may confess in our creeds, have
diminished belief in the transcendent power and utter Godness of the Creator
Spirit, and have become engrossed in our own subjectivities and the development of our own inherent potentialities. Hence the first thing that must
happen to us is a glad subjection to the lordly freedom and majesty of God the
Holy Spirit, and a humble readiness for miraculous divine acts that transcend
all human possibilities and break through the limitations of anything we can
conceive. Come Creator Spirit, is a prayer of open surrender to the absolute
creativity of God.[1]

Who is the One who now fills and transforms Jesus' disciples for
participation in the ministry of reconciliation? The following
pages will highlight three prominent characteristics of the
Spirit and the specific implications for each of these characteristics in the
work of reconciliation. Though many more qualities could be explored, for
the purpose of this book the focus will be on God's Spirit as 1) universal; 2)
creative and personal; and 3) the breath and source of life. In light of these

1. Torrance, *Theology in Reconstruction*, 245.

characteristics of the Spirit the following questions will be addressed: What does it mean to honor the Holy Spirit as God and to allow the Spirit to unite us with God and with others? Under the guidance of the Spirit, what is the scope and shape of that unity? Probing these questions will create a basis from which we can explore, in a subsequent chapter, the role of the imagination in the Spirit's effecting God's will for reconciliation.

Who Is the Holy Spirit and What Shape Does the Spirit Give to Reconciliation?

Until recently, the majority of students in every class I teach at our small evangelical university were raised with very little teaching on the Trinity or the Holy Spirit. The "trinity" holding students' expressed faith loyalty would most often be the Father, the Son, and the Bible. Often their approach to faith development was to find people like themselves who could reinforce their views on Scripture, remind them often of Jesus' death on the cross to forgive their sins, and encourage them to approach decision making by asking, "What would Jesus do?" or WWJD. Failing to do what Jesus would do was not a grave problem, though, since the gospel for them was mostly about forgiveness of sins. This approach, they believed, would ensure that as part of the elect, they would dwell eternally in heaven with a God whose wrath had been appeased by Jesus' death. They evidenced the broader problems in much of Western theology of the results of diminished attentiveness to God the Holy Spirit—problems of cheap grace, weak discipleship, and a narrow understanding of salvation.

In addition to these problems, such a theological approach in Western theology has fueled distorted approaches to the missionary enterprise. As the Greek Orthodox theologian Petros Vassiliadis writes, the Western church has been primarily Christocentric, with Christians going out to convert and conquer the unbelieving world for Christ. At times this has led "to christomonistic imperialism and oppressive expansionism."[2] Japanese theologian Kosuke Koyama describes this as a "crusading mind" rather than a "crucified mind."[3] A diminished sense of God the Spirit can blind Christians to God's creative work and presence among all peoples and can warp mission into conquest and forced assimilation rather than authentic relations.

2. Vassiliadis, "Reconciliation as a Pneumatological Mission Paradigm," 31
3. Koyama, *Water Buffalo Theology*, 32.

Universal in Scope

One of the central affirmations of the church throughout history is that the Holy Spirit is fully God. Thus the Spirit is not an inferior being to God, but rather is God, and therefore universal and infinite in nature and scope. The Spirit does not just appear in the third act of the biblical story, but is present in the birthing of creation in Genesis 1, as well as throughout the Old Testament narrative. Thus, as Clark Pinnock suggests, rather than viewing the Spirit as merely applying the work of Christ to the church in the world, a more robust pneumatology recognizes the universal nature of the "twin interdependent missions of the Son and Spirit."[4] The Son is conceived by the Holy Spirit to further God's mission, which was universal from the beginning.

> The incarnation should not be viewed as a negation of universality but as the fulfillment of what Spirit had been doing all along. The birth of Jesus by the Spirit was the climax of a universal set of operations. Hovering over Mary, Spirit was engaged in new creation. The incarnation marked a new stage in Spirit's universal operations. Spirit, everywhere at work in the whole of history, was now at work in Jesus to make him the head of a new humanity. Throughout history the Spirit has been seeking to create such an impression of God's true self in human beings and hear the response to God that would delight his heart. This is what happened in Jesus by the Spirit. The invisible became visible, and a yes was heard on behalf of the race. . . . The Spirit filled Jesus without measure and opened up the possibility for us to share this fullness. The floodgates of grace were opened for the world.[5]

As Pinnock writes, acknowledging the interdependent missions of Son and Spirit "reduces tension between universality and particularity and fosters a sense that they are complementary rather than contradictory. The two poles turn out to be both-and, not either-or." He goes on to say, "Christ, the only mediator, sustains particularity, while Spirit, the presence of God everywhere, safeguards universality. . . . Because Spirit works everywhere in advance of the church's mission, preparing the way for Christ, God's will can be truly and credibly universal."[6] Thus, the interdependent ministries of the Spirit and the Son call for emphasis both on God's universal mission

---

4. Pinnock, *Flame of Love*, 192.

5. Ibid., 196.

6. Ibid., 192.

as well as God's particular rooting of that mission in Christ. "On the one hand, the Son's mission presupposes the Spirit's—Jesus was conceived and empowered by the Spirit. On the other hand, the mission of the Spirit is oriented to the goals of incarnation. The Spirit's mission is to bring history to completion and fulfillment in Christ."[7]

The mutual emphasis on the particular and the universal is also evident in God's relationship to Israel. As mentioned earlier, Christopher Wright notes that even prior to Jesus Christ, God's particular choice of Abraham and Israel reflect universal vision and a "fresh start for the world."[8] Through them God would extend God's blessings to all the nations. Marc Gopin, an orthodox rabbi, writes,

> Abraham, the father of the Hebrew people, but also the tradi-
> tional father of Islamic peoples and an important figure of faith
> in Christian tradition, is singular in his peculiar relationship to
> God. At the same time, however, with all of his distinct rites and
> ceremonies and his unique story line, he is also a man through
> whom all nations will be blessed (Gen 12:3) and who follows the
> ways of God which involved a universal commitment to justice
> and righteousness. The latter are expressed truly in their most
> radically universalist sense, because Abraham will use these very
> Divine characteristics to defend even the most vile community
> of rapists and murderers in Sodom, demanding before God that
> the innocent should never be swept away with the guilty (Gen
> 18:22–33). . . . Thus it is out of a place of *particularity*, of being a
> sojourner who nevertheless crosses boundaries with a universal
> concern, that Abraham presents an ideal model of engagement
> with the world, without consuming that world or allowing it to
> consume him.[9]

The universal nature of God's grace is evident in the promise that God's presence through the Spirit will be poured out on all people. "We can't miss the universality in this outpouring, for Joel expands his initial phrase 'all people' in three remarkable ways. It will be on men and women (sons *and* daughters). It will be on old and young. And it will even be on slaves, male and female. In other words, there will be no privileged distinctions among God's people as regards who gets the Spirit—no distinctions of gender, age, or class. All will have equal access to sharing in the outpouring

7. Ibid., 194.

8. Wright, *Knowing the Holy Spirit*, 98.

9. Gopin, "The Heart of the Stranger," 13.

that is promised."[10] Similarly, in Acts 3:20–21, Peter affirms God's purpose for "universal restoration that God announced long ago through his holy prophets."

Alan Torrance explains the universal reconciling movement of the Spirit in the following way: "Through the presence of the Spirit, the *koinonia* or communion that God establishes with humanity engenders communion at the 'horizontal' level not only among Christians but between Christians and non-Christians and hopefully, therefore, within the secular world itself. God was in Christ reconciling not some hermetically sealed church but the world."[11]

The universal scope of the Spirit's work extends to all people and to all aspects of our lives to shape people that reflect the very life of Christ. "The outpouring of the Holy Spirit on all of creation meets us in all we do, even in our limitations, sins, and failures."[12] This outpouring is not a generic watering of whatever "spiritual" life might be in evidence, but one that nurtures human responses that resemble Christ's way, truth, and life. In the DNA of the seed that is planted and nourished to life by the Holy Spirit is the cruciform shape of Christ's life—self-giving love in which Christ binds himself to the other. This becomes the source of lasting communal life with God and others. Jesus taught that the Spirit would come and remind us of all that he taught. "When the Spirit of truth comes, he will guide you into all the truth; for he will not speak on his own, but will speak whatever he hears, and he will declare to you the things that are to come. He will glorify me, because he will take what is mine and declare it to you. All that the Father has is mine. For this reason I said that he will take what is mine and declare it to you" (John 16:13–15). The Spirit is described as an advocate whose work is in complete harmony with Jesus' advocacy.

Even as there is a danger of Christomonism,[13] discussions of the universality of the Spirit can veer towards pneumatomonism. As Syriac Orthodox Bishop George Matthew Nalunnakkal notes, "invoking the Spirit without reference to Jesus Christ can lead, in certain cases, to a militant form of pneumato-monism' (viewing the Godhead only in terms of the

---

10. Wright, *Knowing the Holy Spirit*, 150–51. See also Galatians 3:28–29. For more on the universal nature of God's purpose for humankind see DeYoung, *Coming Together in the 21st Century*, 7–12.

11. A. Torrance, "The Theological Grounds for Advocating Forgiveness," 47.

12. Groody, *Globalization*, 231.

13. Barth writes, "Christomonism is excluded by the very meaning and goal of God's and man's union in Jesus Christ." "A Theological Dialogue," 172.

Holy Spirit), as often expressed in some forms of sectarian church tradition, and in some other cases, to a syncretic use of the Spirit."[14]

Thus it is important when thinking of the role of the Spirit to distinguish spirituality in general from Christlike spirituality, which the Spirit fosters. As Groody writes, "While spirituality in general deals with what people most value, Christian spirituality involves living out what Jesus most valued. In other words Christian spirituality is about following Jesus, living out the values of the Kingdom of God, and generating a community transformed by the love of God and others. Expressed in its personal and public dimensions, Christian spirituality is the way in which the invisible heart of God is made visible to the world."[15] Similarly, Jack Levison comments, "filling with the spirit is the way in which the values of the gospel are concretized, the means by which the presence of Jesus is embodied in the world."[16]

As Pinnock writes, God reaches out to all people through the Spirit to foster faithfulness to Christ. "God reaches out to sinners in a multiplicity of ways, thanks to the provenience of the Spirit. God loves sinners, and the Spirit works in them that they may ultimately become obedient to Jesus Christ. . . . Instead of saying there is no salvation outside the church, let us simply say there is no salvation outside grace, or only finally outside Christ."[17]

Thus, when Christians gather around the Eucharist, where as Brueggemann says our "shaloming" begins, it is to remember the depth of God's love for sinners out of which Christ has bound himself to us, and to reenvision the extensiveness of that love reaching out by the Spirit to all people. It is important to acknowledge that salvation is linked with the process of reconciliation that will ultimately culminate at the wedding feast of Christ and his bride in the kingdom of God, with a great multitude flowing from "every nation, from all tribes and peoples and languages" (Rev 7:9). Eucharistic feasts proleptically point to that kingdom feast, drawing people together around Christ, who has bound himself to all people through his flesh and blood and who sends them out from the table by the Holy Spirit to make the new creation visible to all.

14. Nalunnakkal, "Come Holy Spirit," 12.

15. Groody, *Globalization*, 240–41.

16. Levison, *Filled with the Spirit*, 269.

17. Pinnock, *Flame of Love*, 194.

The theme of the 2005 World Council of Churches conference in Athens preserved this paired focus on the Holy Spirit and Christ: "Come Holy Spirit, heal and reconcile: called in Christ to be reconciling and healing communities."[18] Without a focus on the Son, an emphasis on the Spirit can deepen the divisions, and exploit differences to create walls between people rather than to enrich and enhance the multiform unity in Christ for which we were created. It can create contexts in which tolerance is confused for love, and differences are used as an excuse to ignore rather than to love and be bound to one's neighbor. The good news means being joined together in Christ by the Holy Spirit to love and worship the Father through our pluriform ways. To affirm diversity, while ignoring the call and gift of being united together in Christ, is a betrayal of the gospel of reconciliation. In other words, the gospel celebrates the rich diversity of God's creation as it is brought into a resonant harmony in Christ, rather than exalting or being resigned to a multitude of competing tunes, with some drowning others out.

Willie James Jennings poignantly describes the cost of a lack of emphasis on union in Christ, which was evident in much of the colonialist movement. "Christianity in the colonialist moment offers one a gospel that is for everyone of necessity but joins no one of necessity. Thus the incarnation in this order of things comes to signify divine entrance into the world. The specific contours of that entrance lose their social and political character."[19]

As N. T. Wright points out, this is a distortion of the holistic message of the gospel. Thus he asserts, "It is time, and long past time, to reread the gospels as what we can only call political theology—not because they are not after all about God and spirituality and new birth and holiness and all the rest, but precisely because they are."[20]

Acknowledging that the Holy Spirit is God and works universally in ways that honor and lead to Christ-shaped and united life, ministries of reconciliation will gain impetus from seeking to discern what it is that the Spirit is doing in various contexts and communities. "The Spirit's work is not limited to Jews and Christians. God is truly 'the Savior of all people,

18. Vassiliadis, "Reconciliation as a Pneumatological Mission Paradigm," 32.

19. Jennings, *Christian Imagination*, 166. See Jennings's description of John William Colenso's missionary work in what is now South Africa for an illuminating illustration of this very problematic approach in *Christian Imagination*, 119–68.

20. Wright, *How God Became King*, 140.

especially of those who believe' (1 Tim 4:10). Peter says, 'God shows no partiality, but in every nation anyone who fears him and does what is right is acceptable to him' (Acts 10:34–35).[21] Paul quotes Isaiah in acknowledgement of this universal work of God.

> "Their voice has gone out to all the earth,
> and their words to the ends of the world . . .
> I have found those who did not seek me;
> I have shown myself to those who did not ask for me" (Rom 10:18, 20).

Examples of those of outside Israel being anointed with the Spirit include individuals like Cornelius in Acts 10 and Balaam in Numbers 22–24. "So then as early as the time of Israel in the wilderness we find a lesson of what happens when someone exercises prophetic gifts under the control of the Spirit of God. They have a compulsion to speak the truth—even if they come out of a pagan background."[22]

It is precisely because reconciliation is first and foremost the work of God and only secondarily something in which humans participate, that its universal inclusiveness is ensured.[23] Theories of reconciliation that attempt to exclude this vertical and most prominent dimension risk ignoring the infinite reservoir from which the healing waters of reconciliation flow. Though more will be said on this later, it is vital to mention now in order to clarify the importance of acknowledging the universal scope of God the Spirit. Affirming the universality of the Spirit's presence and work is not to encourage a confusion of our human spirits with the Holy Spirit. As Barth states, "if the Holy Spirit is the Spirit of Christ or of the Word, then he, for this reason, cannot be the unblest Spirit of our own working."[24] The Spirit points to and applies the "once for all" nature of Christ's atonement in ways that avoid creating an ethic of reconciliation and a theology of repentance which "are too weak to bear what is loaded upon them."[25]

---

21. Pinnock, *Flame of Love*, 195.

22. Wright, *Knowing the Holy Spirit*, 79.

23. Cf. Schwöbel: "This theocentric emphasis underlies the universality of reconciliation." "Reconciliation," 16.

24. Barth, *The Holy Spirit and the Christian Life*, 26. For more insight into the contrast between "the Spirit of the World and the Spirit from God" see Levison, *Filled with the Spirit*, 279–83. See also John 14:17.

25. Gunton, "Introduction," *The Theology of Reconciliation*, 7.

Creative and Personal

Recognition of the universal scope of the Spirit is vital for ministries in determining which approaches to take and which questions are vital for Christ's ambassadors of reconciliation. The question changes from "What would Jesus do?," which fails to emphasize Jesus' resurrection and presence by his Spirit in the world right now. Instead, a more helpful question is, "What has Jesus Christ been doing through the Spirit among these various individuals and peoples, and what is he doing right now?" The nature of God's Spirit as creative, working in particular as well as universal ways, calls for great attentiveness to see the distinctive things the Spirit may be doing in any given context.

The creative nature of the Spirit is evident throughout the Bible. Creation itself flows from the incubating presence of the Spirit, "hovering over the waters" (Gen 1:2). Thus, as Indian theologian Ivan Satyavrata writes, "All of creation reflects the creative presence and power of the Spirit."[26] It follows that artistic creativity itself flows from the power of the Holy Spirit. As Shirley Guthrie points out, "In the Old Testament the Spirit of God is the source of all human culture, art, creativity and wisdom (Exod 31:1–6; 35:31; Job 32:9; Dan 1:17)."[27] When the Spirit comes upon Bezaleel, he is filled with "the *ruach* of God, with ability, with intelligence, with knowledge, and with all craftsmanship (Exod 31:3)." The Spirit's work includes artistry, imagination, and skillfulness. God fills those who are to make Aaron's priestly garments with a "ruach of wisdom" (Exod 28:3). The creative work of the Spirit as part of the self-donating love of God includes bringing to form those things of beauty, goodness, and truth that reflect God's nature and point to God's ultimate beauty, goodness, and truth.[28]

Thus Kallistos Ware challenges flattened notions of God's creative work in the beginning, which would disconnect the reality of God creating out of nothing from the essence of God's nature as love. "Rather than say that [God] created the universe out of nothing, we should say that he created it out of his own self, which is love. We should think, not of God the Manufacturer or God the Craftsman, but of God the Lover. Creation

---

26. Satyavrata, *The Holy Spirit*, 55.

27. Guthrie, *Christian Doctrine*, 293.

28. This includes God's creative approach to God's enemies. As Volf notes, "God does not abandon the godless to their evil but gives the divine self for them in order to receive them into divine communion through atonement, so also should we—whoever our enemies and whoever we may be." *Exclusion and Embrace*, 23.

is an act not so much of his free will as of his *free love*."[29] The Spirit not only incubates the life that overflows from love, but sustains that life so it can retain its true essence in reflecting back a loving response to God and overflowing in creativity.

Qualities of Reconciliation that Flow from the Spirit's Nature as Creative and Personal

What is our response to the creative nature of the Holy Spirit, specifically in reference to participation in God's reconciling ways? I would suggest that the creative nature of the Holy Spirit overflowing from God's love calls forth three responses: determined avoidance of formulaic approaches to reconciliation; eager openness to the new creation God is bringing; and faithful adherence to God rather than to systems of self-aggrandizement and control. Though such an approach requires acceptance of vulnerability, it also is essential for the serendipitous and creative path to healing that the Holy Spirit offers.[30]

AVOIDANCE OF FORMULAIC APPROACHES

As people who seek control and security through human-centered approaches, our tendency is to try to develop "five steps to bring peace" that can be applied uniformly and universally. Thus one can avoid the ongoing vulnerability demanded in relying on God as the Reconciler and in relating to the real human lives involved. Though God's love and reach are universal through the Spirit, God's ways are pluriform and personalized in rich creativity.[31]

As Schreiter conveys, Jesus demonstrates such particularized approaches in his Resurrection appearances. "*Jesus appears as he needs to be seen.* The purpose of the appearances is not to make a point or to establish a fact. It is to heal, to reconcile. Each of Jesus' appearances . . . is to reestablish

---

29. Ware, *Orthodox Way*, 44.

30. See, for example, Lederach's call for an adaptive and creative approach to peace building, which like a spider weaves a web in a variety of places, yet creates many points of interconnectedness: "Strategic peacebuilders do not confuse the more permanent nature of purpose with the far more fluid nature of responsive innovation and the forms it must take." *Moral Imagination*, 127.

31. See Campbell, "Reconciliation in Paul," 45.

a relationship, to confirm a bond of trust, to touch and heal a broken heart. The mode and manner of Jesus' appearances are shaped to the needs of those who come to recognize who he is."[32]

Thus to participate in God's reconciling ways by the Spirit may mean that the seeds of our own preconceived agendas and programs must fall to the ground and die before a harvest of peace can emerge. As John Paul Lederach writes, "The strength of our processes of change . . . will depend on our capacity to innovate, imagine alternatives, and adapt to shifting sands while sustaining our goal in mind."[33]

Participating in Jesus' personalized approaches to reconciliation calls for the willingness to probe the particularities of God's work in each context, to have established relationships in the context, and thus to develop responses according to careful prayer and observation. The unifying goal of adoption into Christ for all people remains constant, but the way that goal is achieved varies.

As Gopin writes, "We cannot enter as peacemakers into a culture or a religious society with a pre-programmed, homogenized set of values and principles, unless those principles are accompanied by an embrace of the unique identity of groups and individuals. . . . It requires us to express the depth of identity, including religious identity, in a way that embraces its own uniqueness but also shares with the whole society a set of shared meanings."[34]

Overcoming the tendency to rely on the security of familiar approaches and formulaic patterns requires a willingness to trust the Holy Spirit deeply and to be willing to wait on the Spirit's guidance and creativity. It demands the humility to listen to what God is already doing in that context. Jesus promises that his sheep will hear his voice so they may follow him (John 10:27).[35] Such humble attentiveness is connected with the ability to face issues within oneself and one's own community in terms of broken relationships, and recognition of the long-term process necessary for true healing of relationships.

32. Schreiter, *Ministry of Reconciliation*, 48.

33. Lederach, *Moral Imagination*, 119.

34. Gopin, "Heart of the Stranger," 16. In *The Christian Imagination,* Jennings points out the "pedagogical nightmare" that ensued when missionary enterprises assumed an assimilationist approach that either denigrated the particularities of indigenous cultures (114) or disregarded them as having any theological import (147).

35. For more on the vital need for humility in discerning the Spirit's guidance see Smith, *The Voice of Jesus*, 72.

Thus, for example, it is not surprising that student or church groups have a difficult time when they travel to Rwanda to help with two-week-long reconciliation workshops, without an extensive season of prayer, without ever having dealt with the immense divisions in their own lives, cities, and churches, and without having spent much time getting to know people or the history of conflict in Rwanda. People often return from such trips feeling deeply disillusioned about the weak impact of their efforts, having hoped somehow to address the wounds of decades. Since God is the reconciler in Christ and it is by the Holy Spirit that reconciliation can be experienced and effected, we are offered richer and more appropriate ways to experience and convey the wonder of God's very personalized power in and through our lives in the ministry of reconciliation.

OPENNESS TO THE NEW CREATION GOD IS BRINGING

Robert Schreiter describes unexpected "moments of grace" as a key element of the reconciliation process.[36] "The moment of grace is precisely that—a moment of grace, when suddenly the perspective shifts, a new meaning is found, and a pathway appears, leading out of the deep tangle of memories, emotions, and stories of death."[37] This is not something that can be planned or constructed but comes from God's creative work to heal and restore, and serves as a "window onto the eternal."[38] To acknowledge reconciliation as the gift of God includes the willingness to pray and wait openly for this more expansive "window onto God's purposes for us, for the one being healed."[39] Schreiter connects this gift of newness with God's presence and God's perspective.

John Paul Lederach conveys this new creation by God as a seren-dipitous sudden turning, hiddenness like yeast that bubbles forth.[40] Such was the case for Angelina Atyam, whom I met in Burundi a few years ago. Angelina lives in the northern region of Uganda and suffered the abduction of her daughter with a number of other Aboke schoolgirls by Joseph Kony, of the Lord's Resistance Army. Kony held her daughter as a prisoner for more than seven years. During those years, Angelina gathered together

36. Schreiter, *Ministry of Reconciliation*, 46.
37. Ibid.
38. Ibid., 48.
39. Ibid., 50.
40. Lederach, *Moral Imagination*, 113–29.

other parents of abducted children and formed the Concerned Parents' Association, which prayed together weekly for their children. Her advocacy became so well-known that she was invited to speak at the United Nations and was given the 1998 UN Prize for Activism in Human Rights.

Angelina described a time in which she pled with God for her daughter and all the children, and deeply wrestled with God to fulfill God's promise of a seventh-year release of all slaves. When they closed the Concerned Parents' meeting with the Lord's Prayer, God spoke to her, challenging her to forgive her debtors even as God had forgiven her debts. Suddenly, Angelina realized she had not forgiven the captors, and she felt called to let go of her bitterness. She traveled to meet with the mother of the general holding her daughter captive and offered her forgiveness. Angelina has awakened to her identity as a new creation who now leads others who have suffered in the Congo, Burundi, Uganda, and Kenya to experience God's renewing life through the Spirit's gift of forgiveness. She is careful to emphasize the difference between forgiveness and reconciliation, since reconciliation cannot occur without repentance and some form of justice. But she also helps people to experience freedom in their context by drawing them into God's surprising ways of breaking the chains of hatred, bitterness, and despair, and empowering them to trust and to let go.[41]

ADHERENCE TO GOD RATHER THAN TO SYSTEMS OF SELF-AGGRANDIZEMENT AND CONTROL

Openness to the Spirit's creativity in reconciliation requires deep reliance on God and trust that God's ways are higher than our ways (Isa 55:8). This includes a willingness to relinquish comfort and control in what Brueggemann calls our "settled arrangements."[42] As he points out in *Living Toward the Common Good*, such systems of control are established to benefit some and exploit others, and they produce a society sickened with anxiety at all

---

41. Angelina Atyam's story is described at greater length in Katongole, *The Sacrifice of Africa*, 148–65. Joseph Liechty describes "letting go" as the first strand in the process of forgiving, specifically letting go of "vengeance, punishment of the wrongdoer in exact proportion to the wrong done, and in so far as possible, those feelings, especially hatred, that will damage, immediately or eventually, the wronged party." Letting go does not include letting go of the justice claim that occasioned the need for forgiveness, but it is a way of dealing with that justice claim. Liechty, "Putting Forgiveness in its Place," 61–62.

42. Brueggemann, *Spirituality of the Psalms*, 64.

levels.[43] God's people were liberated from Pharaoh's imperial system so that they would learn to live for the common good through trusting in God's provision for all in their midst. Their departure from that system "is a piece of demanding, sustained work. The capacity to think and imagine and act and live beyond that system requires imagination that has dimensions of the psychological, the economic, and the liturgical."[44] It is the thesis of this book that the Holy Spirit is the source of power to reimagine life and to live for the common good, without whom God's people can quickly default to systems of fearfulness and greed.

For those who like control and who benefit from maintaining the present order, the Spirit of God is a threat and a voice to be muted. As Moltmann writes, Spirit-impelled movements "became a danger to the patriarchy, the men's church and the slave-owners."[45] This in turn threatens the movement toward reconciliation, which requires dying to old, static identities and systems of control, and being raised and newly created by the Spirit of Resurrection in Christ.

The impact of Mozart's music being diffused throughout Shawshank prison (in the movie *Shawshank Redemption*) by a prisoner named Andy Dufresne provides a helpful analogy of the impact of the Holy Spirit being poured out on a community. As Andy risked broadcasting his beloved music to the entire prison through the warden's sound system, most prisoners are entranced, "opened up," drawn into a unified gaze and awe at the wonder of this liberating beauty entering in, "like some beautiful bird flapped its wings into our drab little cage . . . and for a minute, every man in Shawshank felt free."[46] But the chief warden is outraged, commanding Andy to turn it off and breaking an office window to halt this liberating experience that threatens his complete control. In contrast, Andy has received the music as a gift of hope and joy to which he holds fast even when thrust into solitary confinement. In this music he experiences a moment of grace and hopeful remembering, which frees him to extend grace to the entire prison at great personal cost. Not so for those who prefer security and control.

---

43. Brueggemann describes the ways in which such self-elevating systems are exemplified by the ancient Pharaoh, who is the "paradigmatic enemy of the common good," and whose approach "produces anxiety that affects every dimension of the system." *Living Toward the Common Good*, 3.

44. Ibid., 30.

45. Moltmann, *Source of Life*, 23.

46. Morgan Freeman's character in *Shawshank Redemption*.

It is not surprising that artists are some of the key change agents of societies, and those who are most quickly silenced when totalitarian regimes want to maintain a firm grasp on power. Hisham Matar, a Libyan writer, expressed this powerfully. "Dictatorship by its essence is interested in one narrative, [an] intolerant narrative, and writers are interested in a multiplicity of narratives and conflicting empathies and what it would be like to be the other, to imagine what the other is thinking and feeling," Matar says. "And that sort of completely unsettles the dictatorial project."[47]

Hans Urs von Balthasar writes of the artistic nature of those whom God chose as change agents in Israel: "God needs prophets in order to make himself known, and all prophets are necessarily artistic."[48] Not all artists are prophets advocating for God-inspired changes, but where the Spirit of the Lord is, there is newness of life that reflects God's desire to draw all people in, to experience God's transforming love and become self-giving reflections of divine life.[49] This newness of life has a penetrating effect on peoples and cultures and exposes the absurdity of the lie that God's grace is reserved for those who some deem superior or more powerful, a claim as absurd as the idea that the sun and the rain are reserved for only a select few.[50]

Maggy Barankitse of Burundi evidences adherence to God and creative resistance to systems of control on behalf of all in her community. Rather than capitulate to fellow Tutsis when they came to kill all the Hutus at the bishop's compound where she worked, she hid as many children as possible and refused to collaborate in identifying the Hutus from the Tutsis. She knew that God's love was for all people and held fast to her faith even when she was stripped, humiliated, and forced to watch the executions of those whom she loved. She claimed the forgiving, universal love of God when she transformed that place of killing into numerous homes for orphans from both ethnic groups. She renamed this site of massacre and enmity "Maison Shalom." She drew on the creative Spirit of God when she prayerfully considered what would help the children to experience their

47. Hisham Matar, "Hisham Matar On The Power Of Libyan Fiction."

48. Von Balthasar, *The Glory of the Lord*, vol. 1, 43. See also Volf on salvation and renaming and remaking in *Exclusion and Embrace*, ch. 3.

49. For insight on the way salvation extends beyond mere liberation to a transformation that empowers self–giving love, see Volf, *Exclusion and Embrace*, 101–5. He qualifies this, however, as an emphasis on love that does not "mean abandoning the project of liberation," but including and transforming even it (105).

50. See Matthew 5:45.

own dignity as royal sons and daughters of the King of kings. Thus she built a lovely flower garden, a chapel, a swimming pool, a movie theater, shops where children could learn specific vocational skills, and she provided ways for the children to retain their cultural distinctives in music, dance, and drumming. Daily prayer in the chapel, inscribed with Jesus' beatitudes, roots her life in the Spirit's outpouring of strong and courageous love. Maggie gave up her own family land to build a hospital for all the people in her region. She acts on her vision of the kingdom of God, and calls others to dream God's dreams with her.[51]

The Character of the Holy Spirit's Creativity that Distinguishes it from Other 'Spirits' of Creativity

Yet, how does one know which creative work and what new movements are of the Holy Spirit? Are there some "controls" needed to maintain fidelity to the truth of God's self-revelation? Specifically in relation to the ministry of reconciliation, Barth's description of the Spirit's creative work is particularly apt. The Spirit's nurturing presence with humans makes them "opened, prepared, and made fit by God for God."[52] Openness to God's voice and ways is essential if we are to participate in God's ministry of reconciliation, for "The created spirit is in no wise 'open upward' in itself: it is not within the compass of any cleverness or ability of mind, but it is purely and simply the office of the Holy Spirit to be continually opening our ears to enable us to receive the Creator's word."[53] The question continually arises, then, does a new creative work of the Spirit align with the Creator's living word in Jesus and written word in the Bible? And if so, how do we remain open to see and hear and align ourselves with this new work of the Spirit? Openness calls for a posture more like clay to the potter's hands (Jer 18), like a maid waiting on her mistress, or servants on their master (Ps 123). As F. K. Schumann wrote, "As a creature I know that I am being created ever anew, in the advance from one moment to the next moment: ever anew as not

---

51. Maggy Barankitse, the 2008 Opus Prize winner, was a featured speaker at Duke's African Great Lakes Initiative 2010 in Burundi, which the author of this book attended. (January 12–15, 2010, Bujumbura, Burundi.)

52. Barth, *Holy Spirit and the Christian Life*, 7.

53. Ibid., 8.

capable of managing myself, ever anew as one placed in the unknown, ever again being delivered into a strange Hand."[54]

This calls for eschewing human-centered and self-serving notions of reconciliation ("forgive and forget" or "let bygones be bygones").[55] Without the work of the Spirit to turn us "away from ourselves such that we are brought to think from a center outside us," to live "*ex curvatus ex se*," our efforts can ultimately end up silencing and muting the voices of the violated rather than opening them up.[56] At times self-serving efforts to force unity without justice and call it reconciliation have made the word itself seem vile and offensive. Such efforts have stifled the new creative movement of the Spirit. In Rwanda, for example, "the 'r' word, 'reconciliation,' was taboo for several years after the 1994 genocide against Tutsis."[57] In other more socially stable contexts, reconciliation has been used in a numbing way, as Rowan Williams writes, "a seductively comfortable word, fatally close to 'consensus.'"[58]

In a radical challenge to closed and stifling systems, Barth proclaims, theological "ethics has to serve the Word of God, even as theology should. It must not anticipate that Word, nor may it obstruct that Word by setting up a human law."[59] Instead Christian ethics calls for receptivity to the Holy Spirit, who makes it possible for Christ's sheep to hear his voice and follow in his way.

---

54. Friedrich Karl Schumann, *Der Gottesgedanke and der Zerfall der Moderne,* 360, in Barth, *Holy Spirit and the Christian Life,* 16–17.

55. "The form of life that [God] prescribes and seeks to engender is an intentionality that, by its very nature, we *cannot* achieve through the introverted actions of oneself upon oneself. It is neither subjectively manufactured nor self-determined but *generated* in and through an event wherein the Spirit directs us to perceive the unanticipatable, historical Self-giving of God to which the Incarnation testifies and that the self-same presence of the Spirit embodies." A. Torrance, "The Theological Grounds for Advocating Forgiveness," 50.

56. Ibid.

57. Gobodo-Madikizela, *A Human Being Died That Night,* 124. See also De Gruchy on Botha's use of the term "reconciliation" to "perpetuate the regime's control and hegemony in a new guise." *Reconciliation,* 34.

58. Williams, *On Christian Theology,* 266. The point is not to eschew tradition, but to allow God's Spirit and Word to continually reshape and remold the clay pots of tradition to correlate more with the kingdom of God and less with rigid and self-serving fortresses. MacDonald depicts the life and soul-crushing nature of such religious rigidity in his book *Phantastes,* 171–74.

59. Barth, *Holy Spirit and the Christian Life,* 9.

The Holy Spirit creates a way by which humans can both hear and do the will of God. As Augustine writes, "But the Holy Spirit works within us to make the medicine work that is applied to us from without."[60] Barth comments that we are able to hear the Spirit speak through action and prayer in a way that miraculously moves us from "human vanity" to "divine truth."[61] This includes honoring the power of the Holy Spirit to reveal truth in particularized and creative ways that challenge dominant cultural understandings, not least the tendency to assume evaluative hegemony in determining what is of God and what is not.[62] A powerful illustration of this comes from Acts 10, in which the Holy Spirit challenges Peter to let go of deeply held convictions based on centuries of Jewish thought in order to participate in God's reconciliation of Cornelius and his family specifically and Gentiles in general. More on this transformative encounter and issues of discernment will be developed later in this book. "Only in the miracle of the Holy Spirit are [God's commandments] not hidden from us."[63]

The Spirit works moment by moment to mold us into the new creations we are becoming in Christ, people who reflect Christ's nature. The power of the Spirit's creativity is evident as we are transformed from those who are addicted to independence to those who join Jesus in complete dependence on the Father, with such prayerful openness that we may do nothing but what we see the Father doing. The Spirit's creativity is revealed when we become vulnerable, and trust in Jesus that God is sharing all that is needed with God's children.[64]

Schreiter offers an instructive contrast between "vulnerability" and "weakness" that can help "honor-and-shame" cultures to approach forgiveness positively as a strength rather than a weakness. "Forgiving in honor-and-shame cultures may be considered a sign of weakness, but the forgiveness that Jesus preached was forgiveness growing out of love. And genuine love carries with it vulnerability. The difference between vulnerability and weakness is that vulnerability is something freely offered, whereas weakness is an unwanted deficit of power. Vulnerability is a manifestation of the trust that is at the basis of self-giving in love."[65]

---

60. Augustine, *De civitas Dei* 15.6, in Barth, *Holy Spirit and the Christian Life*, 16, n.25.

61. Barth, *Holy Spirit and the Christian Life*, 11.

62. See Jennings, *Christian Imagination*, 112–16.

63. Barth, *Holy Spirit and the Christian Life*, 11.

64. Schreiter, *Ministry of Reconciliation*, 60.

65. Ibid.

The Spirit's creativity is experienced when we die daily to old self-referent ways of thinking and judging, and rise to new life and love in Christ. This becomes the "free space of trust" where "our powers are awakened and new powers grow."[66] Such is the vital transforming work needed if we are to become the kind of peacemakers who are called sons and daughters of God.

Again the creativity of the Spirit ensures that this is no homogenizing transformation, but one that brings out the unique gifts and particularities of each person and community more fully. Levison points out that in contrast to the promise of a new heart to Israel as a whole in Ezekiel 36:26–27, in the new creation, "the spirit is given 'in our heart,' in the hearts of individual believers."[67] As the morning light brings out diverse colors that before dawn are subdued and dim, so the Spirit's light of Christ-transformation brings greater freedom for unique expressions of Christlikeness. As Moltmann writes, "It is only as a unity in diversity that the Christian community will become an inviting community in a society which is otherwise pretty uniform. Creation is motley and diverse, and the new creation even more so."[68]

The Spirit as the Breath and Source of Life

Even as the Spirit is universal in scope and creative in shaping new life, the Spirit is the very breath and source of all that lives. As Moltmann writes, "For the Holy Spirit is 'the source of life' and brings life into the world—whole life, full life, unhindered, indestructible, *everlasting* life. The creative and life-giving Spirit of God already brings this eternally living life here and now, before death, not just after death, because the Spirit brings Christ into this world and Christ is 'the resurrection and the life' in person. . . . The sending of the Holy Spirit is the revelation of God's indestructible *affirmation* of life, and his marvelous *joy* in life."[69] The call for God's people then is to "build up a universal 'culture of life' and resist 'the barbarism of death' wherever we are."[70] The Spirit can blow life even into a valley of dead bones and bring new life, according to Ezekiel 37:1–14.[71]

66. Moltmann, *Source of Life*, 63.

67. Levison, *Filled With the Spirit*, 307–8.

68. Moltmann, *Source of Life*, 60.

69. Ibid., 19.

70. Moltmann citing Pope John II, *Source of Life*, 20.

71. See Levison, *Filled With the Spirit*, Part III, ch. 2, for rich reflections on the connections between Ezekiel 36–37 and Paul's writing on the Spirit.

What Does This Mean Specifically for Those Sharing in the Ministry of Reconciliation?

All Life Is given and Sustained by the Holy Spirit

First of all this means that those who participate in the ministry of reconciliation will recognize that each and every life is a gift sustained by the Holy Spirit. It is not up to any individual to judge another as a lost cause. Even the most twisted life has something of God's life left in him or her, and is to be respected, honored, and treated as a "thou" rather than an "it," as Buber elucidated in *I and Thou*.[72]

One of the powerful themes of Tolkien's *The Lord of the Rings* is that the one being who most obviously "warrants" being eliminated, Gollum, is treated with mercy and an ever-expanding relationship of cautious mutuality, at least by Frodo. The compassion that Bilbo originally showed to Gollum is credited with preventing the usual toxic effect of the ring from poisoning Bilbo as much as it could have. Ultimately the ongoing mercy with which Gollum is approached becomes a key component in saving Middle Earth. Frodo is able to grow in his guarded affection for Gollum because he is increasingly able to see something of himself in Gollum, and to respect the life and struggle that Gollum bears. As will be discussed later, this requires a rich imaginative leap for Frodo—to be able to see Gollum, his enemy, as someone with whom he can identify.

People who have experienced great violence against them are often empowered and freed when they can avoid dehumanizing and hating the perpetrator. This occurs when they can see something of the life of God continuing to pursue the other in even the smallest of ways. Acknowledgement of this shared source of life can keep one from descending into a morass of downward-spiraling relationships. "If we demonize or animalize 'perpetrators,' then we also become guilty of a dehumanization, which typically was a crucial step in making it possible for them to commit the horrible against faceless victims."[73] Thus, South African philosopher Wilhelm Verwoerd describes a mother who lost a child under apartheid challenging others "to demonstrate a humanness [*ubuntu*] towards [perpetrators], so that [it] in turn may restore their own humanity."[74]

---

72. Buber, *I and Thou*.

73. Verwoerd, "Toward Inclusive Remembrance after the 'Troubles,'" 118.

74. Ibid.

Nelson Mandela's ability to see the good in others was a powerful resource for facilitating the transition from an extremely hostile situation to one of cooperation and a sense of shared future, for him personally and for the entire country of South Africa. Richard Strengel writes, "it is not that Mandela does not see the dark side of his enemies, but that he is unwilling to see *only* that. . . . He chooses to look past the negative. He does this for two reasons: because he instinctively sees the good in people and because he intellectually believes that seeing the good in others might actually make them better."[75]

Seeing the good in others is possible as we grasp that we have a shared source of life, identity, purpose, and dignity. God, the source of all life, has created all people in God's image to bring all into mutuality and love as God's own sons and daughters. This kind of seeing requires a work of the Holy Spirit in our imagination, to move us beyond the obvious social, cultural, racial, and economic barriers that would pit us against one another. Thus Norman Wirzba writes, "Once we learn to appreciate our own lives and those around us as gifts from God, we do not need to enter into bitter struggle and inflict various forms of pain and suffering upon each other. The many relations that feed into our being and literally constitute it can now be embraced and celebrated as so many forms of manna from heaven."[76]

A Call to Challenge Notions of Superiority/Inferiority

Second, acknowledging that all life finds it source in God's Holy Spirit challenges the socially fracturing fallacies that some lives are more intrinsically worthy than others. Christians have at times employed notions of chosenness to argue that some people are more highly valued than others. This has been used as a rationalization for colonialism, exploitation, and denigration of indigenous people especially. License to seize land from indigenous peoples (such as in the United States from Native Americans and in Israel from Palestinians) has been rooted in the misunderstanding of chosenness that some people are more valued by God than others.

Gopin specifically challenges the mind-set that equates ancient Israel's election with superiority, and the entire misappropriation of the idea of chosenness. "How anyone in their right mind could have read the Prophets of Israel and come to the conclusion that chosenness meant superiority

75. Strengel, *Mandela's Way*, 118. See also Tutu, *Made for Goodness*.
76. Wirzba, *Living the Sabbath*, 83.

or privilege is beyond me. . . . The number of groups that, in the name of monotheism, have used the chosenness metaphor to destroy indigenous peoples physically or emotionally in the past millennium defies the imagination."[77] Rather than receiving God's blessing as a call to image divine self-giving love in order to bless others, chosenness became an excuse for self-aggrandizement.

Though the Holy Spirit is the author of all life and all people, hierarchical determinations of human worth have been destructively used to establish value based on gender, class, ethnicity, and skin color. These stratifying determinations have been used to structure societies throughout the ages and continue to frame the judgments of people with the power to steer even the most "democratic" of societies.

An example of destructive allocation of value based on class was expressed in a private memo by Lawrence H. Summers when he was under secretary of the US Treasury Department during the Clinton administration. The memo to six influential colleagues, eventually leaked to the press, includes these remarks:

> Just between you and me, shouldn't the World Bank be encouraging *more* migration of the dirty industries to the LDCs (Less Developed Countries)? . . . The measure of the costs of health impairing pollution depends on the foregone earnings from increased morbidity and mortality. From this point of view a given amount of health impairing pollution should be done in the country with the lowest cost, which will be the country with the lowest wages. I think the economic logic behind dumping a load of toxic waste in the lowest wage country is impeccable and we should face up to that.[78]

The "impeccable logic" goes something like this: if we are going to pollute and damage life, it's better if it impacts the lives of those whose earning potential is lower than those who are able to earn more.

---

77. Gopin, "Heart of the Stranger," 14. See also Jennings, *Christian Imagination*, 15–64.

78. Lawrence Summers, "Summers Memo" (1991) in De La Torre, *Doing Christian Ethics from the Margins*, 122. In an effort to diminish the damage from this leaked memo Summers and his assistant Lant Pritchett claimed that he was being sarcastic in this statement. See Johnson et al., "Potential Gains from Trade from Trade in Dirty Industries: Revisiting Lawrence Summers' Memo." For further examples of the use of this type of logic to justify systems of inequality, see Stiglitz, *The Price of Inequality*.

Rather than contributing to greater social harmony and reconciliation, dehumanizing attitudes like this increase experiences of alienation and fragmentation. Fault lines that fracture communities are continually appearing where male babies are valued over female babies (misogyny and gendercide), where light-skinned people are valued over dark-skinned people (pigmentocracy), where youth is valued over age (ageism), and where the able are valued over those who are disabled (ableism).

The Spirit breathes life into and is poured out on all flesh, young and old, male and female, weak and strong. "By the word 'flesh' Joel [2:28–32] means especially 'the weak, the people without power and without hope.'"[79] Life shaped by the Spirit reflects Jesus' teaching, that the last shall be first and the least shall be the greatest of all. The Spirit's anointing thus means "good news to the poor" rather than the dehumanization of those demeaned by social pecking orders.[80] "The Spirit of God is no respecter of social distinctions; it puts an end to them. All Spirit-impelled revival movements in the history of Christianity have taken note of these socially revolutionary elements in the experience of the Spirit and have spread them."[81] Paul Pierson has argued, "Movements of renewal and mission always seem to arise on the periphery of the churchly structures."[82] Pierson encourages people to remember this, for "It will enable you to be more open to the creative new initiatives of the Holy Spirit."[83] One can see examples in the Wesleyan revival among Welsh miners, and the Pentecostal revival among the poor throughout the world. This will be explored more fully in the concluding chapter.

Participation in the Spirit's Nurturing Way Is Integral to the Work of Reconciliation

Third, taking seriously the nature of the Holy Spirit as the source and breathe of life means that the goal within reconciliation ministries is to share in the Spirit's nurturing and life-giving work. When one can identify with the other as someone also created and sustained by God's Spirit, the

79. Wolff, *Joel und Amos* in *Biblischer Kommentar: Altes Testament*, 80, cited by Moltmann, *Source of Life*, 23.

80. Luke 4:18.

81. Moltmann, *Source of Life*, 23.

82. Pierson, *Dynamics of Christian Mission*, 6.

83. Ibid., 40.

urge will more likely be to foster and protect their life. God's Spirit brought creation into being, hovering over the chaos, and new creation into being by hovering over Mary. It is fascinating that the word for mercy in both Arabic and Hebrew derives from the same root word, meaning womb.[84] To share in the Spirit's nature is to create a safe place for life to grow and flourish. In the work of reconciliation it requires drawing close enough to extend a kind of incubating warmth that participates in the Spirit's work of re-creation.

Sometimes this can be as basic as looking into the face of the stranger or enemy and seeking to find there something of the light of the Spirit. Drawing on wisdom from the Torah, Rabbi Gopin writes, "It is as if the Divine voice says perpetually to the inner self who is conscious of the sacred laws of morality, 'You want to find Me? . . . You have only to look and really see the stranger or estranged Other who walks past you every day. And the more that you truly see him or her, the more you will find Me.'"[85]

The transformation that can happen when two people who have been enemies are willing to look closely into each other's faces is conveyed powerfully in the memoir *Picking Cotton*. For eleven years Ronald Cotton was the most despised, hated, and feared man in Jennifer Thompson-Cannino's life. She had succeeded in making sure he was condemned for her rape, and indirectly for the rape of another woman, and given two life sentences plus fifty-five years. Ronald Cotton, who turned out not to be her rapist, had to wait eleven years in various prisons before he received justice through DNA testing that exonerated him. Cotton describes their first face-to-face meeting:

> Sometimes people don't have to say a thing. If you look directly into their eyes, it's all there. People's eyes talk. I learned to read people like that when I was in prison. So it was good to be there, to hear her and see the expressions on her face. I could see that she was truly sorry. It was plain as day: If she could've gone back and turned the hands of time to change what happened, she would have. "I forgive you," I told her. . . . For the first time, in so many years, I didn't see the hate in her eyes. She didn't look at me and see the man who had hurt her, the man she wanted dead, she saw *me*. I didn't even think about it until after the fact, but I reached for her hands and all of a sudden, we were standing there, hugging.[86]

84. Moucarry, *Search for Forgiveness*, 31–2.

85. Gopin, "Heart of the Stranger," 9.

86. Thompson-Cannino and Cotton, *Picking Cotton*, 244–45.

Even though she had imagined him in a way that fostered hatred and his complete destruction, he is able to see her through an imaginative framework that perceives her regret and thus he is able to desire new life and forgiveness for her. He is able to respond in a nurturing and healing manner, rather than seeking vengeful retaliation for the lost years of his life.

Thompson-Cannino describes her experience of this reconciliation in a way that demonstrates the need for a more robust imagination when it comes to the hope of new beginnings and restored relationships: "Another thing that stunned me: how gentle and soft-spoken Ronald Cotton was, nothing like the menacing voice I could still hear hissing in my mind, the voice I had associated with his image for so long. And I had certainly never imagined that he would stand before me and say, 'I forgive you,' just that easily and that simply. He was free, I realized, truly free."[87]

There is something miraculous when one can look into an enemy's eyes and see shared life and humanity. There is something spiritually profound in the transformation of a hate-filled imagination to an imagination that desires to nurture well-being in the one who has been a destructive enemy. Dori Laub experienced this transformation while she participated in the hunting down and killing of Nazi collaborators at the end of World War II. "But when a German youth was captured and brought to her for her to take revenge on him, she ended up caring for him, cleaning and covering his wounds before handing him over as a POW. When asked why she had helped him she replied, 'How could I kill him—he looked into my face and I looked into his.'"[88]

In a book entitled *A Human Being Died that Night*, Pumla Gobodo-Madikizela describes interviews with a man, Eugene de Kock, who was judged to be the face of evil for the apartheid regime. Two women who were widowed because of his actions met with him privately so that he could apologize to them. As they sat face to face one of the women felt "profoundly touched" by him. "Both women felt that de Kock had communicated to them something he felt deeply and had acknowledged their pain. 'I couldn't control my tears. I could hear him, but I was overwhelmed by emotion, and I was just nodding, as a way of saying yes, I forgive you. I hope that when he sees our tears, he knows that they are not only tears for

---

87. Ibid., 249.
88. Laub, "Truth and Testimony," 85.

our husbands, but tears for him as well. . . . I would like to hold him by the hand, and show him that there is a future, and that he can still change.'"[89]

At one point the interviewer, Gobodo-Madikizela, feels such compassion for de Kock that she reaches out to touch him. She is rather stunned and wonders if she has crossed the line from compassion to identification with him. "Hard as the memory of having touched him was, the experience made me realize something I was probably not prepared for—that good and evil exist in our lives, and that evil, like good, is always a possibility. And that was what frightened me."[90]

Sitting down with him, hearing his story, seeing his face, didn't make what he did less horrific, but it did help the glimmers of his humanity to show through both as a hope and a warning. Gobodo-Madikizela felt hope that because of our shared life and humanity no one needs to act as he had. He had had the capacity to choose life and perhaps even now had the capacity to repent and realize what he'd done. Her hope helped her envision the possibility that life could be different in South Africa. "Hope is where transformation begins, without it, a society cannot take its first steps toward reconstructing its self-identity as a society of tolerance and coexistence."[91] At a conference filled with psychoanalysts from North America, the United Kingdom, and South Africa, one man spoke about how important it was "to see these men's humanity, and how much our hope as South Africans depended on reaching out to such glimpses of humanity in a spirit of compassion instead of revenge."[92]

As evident above, drawing close enough to the other to share in the Spirit's life-nurturing role also evokes a warning. The Spirit can help us to identify with the other enough to convict us that the capacity to be life destroyers instead of nurturers is within us all. Thus, as former president Mandela stated, "All of us, as a nation that has newly found itself, share in the shame at the capacity of human beings of any race or language group to be inhumane to other human beings. We should all share in the commitment to a South Africa in which that will never happen again."[93]

---

89. Gobodo-Madikizela, *A Human Being Died,* 14–15.

90. Ibid., 34.

91. Ibid., 126.

92. Ibid., 45.

93. Mandela, *TRC Report,* Vol. I, 134, in Verwoerd, "Toward Inclusive Remembrance," 112.

In this way, the interconnectedness of all of life and of all humans becomes apparent, and strategies to deal with evil become more comprehensive. As the Truth and Reconciliation Report concluded, "We should move away from individual pathology as the explanation for why people commit these gross violations and give much more weight to social identity and 'situationalism', thus appreciating the power of various binding and blinding forces that enable an ordinary person to kill or torture another human being."[94]

The Spirit as life giver is also a source of wisdom and truth to help us face such questions. What is it that shapes a community and society to be so antithetical to the life-giving power of the Holy Spirit? What societal forces and fears blind us to the full humanity of the "others" in our midst and become so much like the air we breathe that we are oblivious to their toxic impact on our lives and communities? How do we come to imagine others as subhuman rather than those who are created in God's image, redeemed in Christ, and sustained by the Holy Spirit? Brenda Salter-McNeil connects these problems with "a spirit of fear that is endemic to society and can be changed only by the Spirit of God."[95]

94. *TRC Report*, Vol. V, 259–303, in Verwoerd, "Toward Inclusive Remembrance," 114.

95. Salter-McNeil, *The Heart of Racial Justice*, 19.

3

Gifts from the Holy Spirit for Reconciliation

Through the captivity of our imagination, God's Spirit draws us forward into the reality of his own future, a future the openness of which is no longer a threat, therefore, but a source of that joyful energy under the influence of which God calls us, for now, to live and labor in the world.[1]

The nature of the Holy Spirit as universal, creative, and the source of life means there are many resources the Spirit offers to deal with painful realities and to bring to fulfillment God's gift of reconciliation. Numerous gifts and fruit of the Holy Spirit, which are particular resources for the ministry of reconciliation, draw on the specific vehicle of the imagination for their expression. Though not an exhaustive list, three areas in particular will be explored as gifts crucial to the healing of relationships, all of which rely heavily on wise imagination: re-creation, hope, and love. Before exploring the specific involvement of the imagination, these three imaginatively rich areas will be clarified in relation to the nature and work of the Spirit.

1. Bauckham and Hart, *Hope against Hope*, 71.

Re-creation

The first of these provisions is the power of the Spirit in re-creation. Of the many dimensions of new creation, three stand out in relation to reconciliation. First, the Spirit leads us from darkness to light, bondage to freedom, alienation to community, and falsehood to truth. Second, the Spirit inspires vibrant diversity in communities while also sustaining deep unity in Christ. Third, the Spirit pours out new vision and imagination to perceive God's presence and work in the world.

Freedom from Darkness, Bondage, Alienation, and Falsehood

In the midst of Paul's most lengthy writing on reconciliation (2 Cor 5:17–21), he writes that if anyone is in Christ, there is a new creation: everything old has passed away. As mentioned previously, the central rites of Christian faith are experiences that draw believers through death into new life. Baptism not only reflects dying with Christ, a cleansing from sin and alienation, but also a new birth in which believers are anointed to live by the creative life of the Holy Spirit. The Eucharist also conveys the invitation for believers to participate in the death and resurrection of Christ and to be nurtured by his life to follow in his new ways.[2] In both there is a sense of new creation that involves corporate transformation, not merely individual change. The new reality conveys inclusion in one universal body with shared life in Christ that is nurtured by the Holy Spirit.[3] As Levison

2. Bishop Desmond Tutu connects the epiklesis of the communion elements with the transformation of God's people. "The principle of transfiguration is actually central to the Christian faith. According to it, something is raised to another and higher level of reality or becomes a channel for communicating that higher level . . . when for instance bread and wine are raised to another level of reality to become the body and blood of Jesus Christ or become the channels for communicating to the recipients the very divine life itself. . . . It is the transfiguration principle at work when an erstwhile persecutor of the Christians can be transformed into the chief of apostles as the apostle to the Gentiles." Michael Battle comments further on Tutu's statement, "Following the tradition of the early church theologians, Tutu believes that whatever the Holy Spirit lays hold of is sanctified and changed, even in the South African context. This view avoids seeing magical powers in doctrines of transubstantiation and ascribes new significance to the doctrine of *pneumatology.*" Michael Battle, *Reconciliation*, 108, citing Tutu from "God who is there."

3. Vassiliadis describes both baptism and Eucharist as significant acts of identity, with Eucharist "celebrated as a manifestation (more precisely a foretaste) of the coming kingdom." And "Baptism is always preceded by a conscious act of repentance, a solemn

writes, "It is not an experience that transpires without a radical revision of reality," but one in which human relationships are restructured. "This is a jarring experience that turns a property owner and his or her property into brothers and sisters, that supplants a spirit of lifelong anxiety with a fresh influx of familial embrace, and that produces a passionate love affair stronger than death."[4]

Even as the first creation involved both "separation and binding," the new creation is ushered in by the Spirit through the power of the Living Word to divide light from darkness, and truth from falsehood.[5] Jesus promised that he would send another Advocate, "the Spirit of truth," who would teach his followers everything and remind them of all he said to them (John 15:26, 14:26). Paul refers to the Spirit in connection with the Word, which he calls the "sword of the Spirit" (Eph 6:17). Included in the Spirit's new creation is the cleaving of what is life-giving from what is destructive, that the truth of the Living Word might set people free.

The Spirit still hovers over the chaos of shadowy places and by the power of the Word of God still brings forth light, and separates the light from the darkness. The sword of the Spirit divides between that which devours and that which reflects God's self-giving love. As the Spirit of God descended on Paul to take the scales off his eyes, so the Spirit can remove sociological blinders from our eyes to astound us with the fact that even the "goyim" are part of God's people and to reveal specific "sacred traditions" of our identity that block the inclusion of others.

The Spirit, in re-creating us, reveals the distortions in our notions of what is bad and what is good. And the Spirit empowers us to relinquish what we had previously grasped and to receive those whom we had previously rejected. For Paul this was the recognition that in the new creation followers of Jesus could let go of the need to be circumcised, in order to welcome the Gentiles more freely. For Peter it was the recognition that God

---

renunciation of the evil and a conscious act of reconciliation, which thus becomes a sign of incorporation into the one body and Spirit (Eph 4:4–5)." Vassiliadis, "Reconciliation as a Pneumatological Mission Paradigm," 40, 41.

4. Levison, *Filled with the Spirit*, 278–79.

5. Volf uses the terms "separating and binding" from the creation narrative to discuss the process of identity formation through both differentiation and connection. He goes on to describe exclusion as transgression against separating and binding. I am positing here that the Spirit's process of leading us into truth (according to Jesus' promise) includes illuminating and empowering God's people toward the healing of relationships, by both revealing and cutting them free from that which is relationally damaging. See Volf, *Exclusion and Embrace*, 65–68.

is the creator of all things; nothing is unclean. For believers throughout the centuries it has meant letting go of traditions that concentrate power and leadership in the church based on skin color, gender, class, and ethnicity.

The Western church has made much of the Spirit's role to convict individuals of their sins, but less of the Spirit's role in exposing and setting God's people free from systemic and communally based sins. The power of the Spirit to recreate a reconciled community from various fractured communities has often been ignored. Cecelia Clegg argues that "Christian churches and faith communities have largely left out of account the social dimension of a theology of reconciliation, preferring to concentrate on the personal dimension." [6] She highlights two effects of this. First, it limits the usefulness of the concept of reconciliation in intergroup conflicts. And second, it impairs Christian visions of creation, salvation, and mission that could speak directly to a fractured world.

One way in which the social dimension of reconciliation can be addressed is to be open to the Spirit cleaving truth from falsehood in the self-promoting biblical interpretations and historical narratives to which we cling. Those seeking to live in the reality of God's work of reconciliation will face the truth of our misuses of the Word to justify social stratification and to block the Spirit's work of cutting away hegemonic structures and perspectives. One example is evident in the Afrikaner church in South Africa. Gobodo-Madikizela describes the way in which a certain view of Scripture was used by President P. W. Botha to encourage the white Afrikaner army in their attacks of black South African townships and their various repressive efforts against demonstrations. A message from him was inscribed inside Bibles given to the South African Army, in Afrikaans: "This Bible is an important part of your calling to duty. When you are overwhelmed with doubt, pain, or when you find yourself wavering, you must turn to this wonderful book for answers. . . . You are now called to play your part in defending our country. It is my prayer that this Bible will be your comfort so that you can fulfill your duty and South Africa and her people will forever be proud of you. Of all the weapons you carry, this is the greatest because it is the Weapon of God." [7]

An unwillingness to allow the sword of the Spirit to clarify such misuses of the gospel and to cut away what is truly evil extends well beyond apartheid-era South Africa. Willie Jennings explores the ways in which

6. Clegg, "Between Embrace and Exclusion," 123.
7. Gobodo-Madikizela, *A Human Being Died that Night*, 59.

an abusive use of the gospel is at the roots and heart of Western culture, and in particular the "Christian social imagination."[8] In the midst of the complex issues and causes for such distortions, one stands out as particularly relevant for the thesis of this book: what Vassiliadis describes as "Christocentric universalism," in which mission was conceived as *mission christianorum*," going out to conquer the world in the name and under the authority of Christ.[9] Jennings describes the way in which Pope Nicolas V's self-identification with Christ created a power base in the fifteenth century from which he, "for the sake of Christ and through Christ, lays claim to the entire world."[10] Connecting himself and his delegate, Prince Henry, to "a trajectory of ownership and salvation" through Christ meant that displacement and enslavement of peoples could be justified as a vehicle of salvation, moving them from godlessness to eternal life in Christ.[11]

The absence of any doctrine of the universal work of the Spirit is evident in the approach to other languages. Jennings writes, "The languages of the newly formed slaves required no hope of a Pentecostal miracle, no need to pray for interpretation, because the imperial reflex on display captured strange tongues and drowned them in the familiar sound of Portuguese."[12] Why honor the languages, cultures, locations, or individuals of these "others" if they are all godless pagans in any case?

Similar distortions of God's new creation are evident in the ways Christians have appropriated the unique narrative of God's people Israel to both exclude Jews from our story and to justify conquest of the New World through our manifest destiny. N. T. Wright argues that in muting the story of God's pilgrimage with Israel, Christians have not only lost a sense of the unique character of the God we worship, but also the wonder of God's ongoing presence with us.[13]

Jennings illustrates this loss through the English hymn writer Isaac Watts's rendering of Psalm 67, in which Watt's describes Britain as the "fav'rite land," God's "chosen isle" blessed by "His choicest favors." As a result, Jennings writes, Watts "mangled the textual mediation of a good word, a word for *all* peoples," and "his supersessionist vernacular loses sight

8. Jennings, *Christian Imagination*, 6, 275, 293.

9. Vassiliadis, "Reconciliation," 36.

10. Jennings, *Christian Imagination,* 26.

11. Ibid., 28.

12. Ibid., 21.

13. Wright, *How God Became King*, 61–81.

of Israel's story and thereby loses sight of the opening of the world to the disclosure of its creator."[14]

The ultimate shift in the dominant paradigms for mission, from *mission christianorum* to *mission ecclesiae* and finally to *mission Dei*, can be seen as the Spirit's way of transforming the church's misguided orientation into one that is more fully centered in the triune God.[15] "It is not that the church of God has a mission in the world, but that the Triune God of mission has a church in the world."[16] In no small measure, the Holy Spirit has spoken through the voices of the dispossessed, the conquered, and disempowered to call for such a change, that the church might more closely reflect the dispossessed, conquered, and yet resurrected one whom it claims to worship.[17] In this way the work of the Spirit in all people and all places may be more fully acknowledged and honored. The Spirit's twofold role in speaking to and through the dispossessed and cleaving away the arrogance of those who claim to possess the truth is pivotal in the movement toward shalom. The Spirit makes us all one, as those who now belong to God, Father, Son, and Holy Spirit.

Rather than an arrogant attitude in which the church moves out to conquer and claim in the name of Christ, the church is called to be attentive and inviting. This means both honoring the presence of God among diverse peoples and participating in the invitation of Father, Son, and Spirit, "drawing humanity and creation in general into this communion with God's very life."[18]

Does the church pray for our scales of arrogance and prejudice to be removed, knowing that the Spirit gives life to all people, and is a defender of the weak and powerless? "Like sin, crime that is a gross violation of human

---

14. Jennings, *Christian Imagination,* 217–19. For further reading see 207–88.

15. Vassiliadis, "Reconciliation," 36.

16. T. Dearborn, *Beyond Duty,* 14. Cf. Jürgen Moltmann: "In its original and eternal sense, mission is God's mission (*missio Dei*). It is only when our Christian mission follows the divine sending and corresponds to it that it is a mission with confidence in God and an assured faith. . . . It is only when we as people follow God's mission to other people and put ourselves in line with that mission that we show respect for the dignity of others, as people created by God and made in his image; and it is only then that we shall resist the temptation to try to dominate them religiously." *Source of Life,* 19.

17. Liberation and global theologians such as Gustavo Guttieriez, James Cone, and Koysuke Koyame have called the Western church to accountability for its hegemonic and destructive approaches of the past, and as the Spirit has opened the ears and eyes of Western Christians, truth has been cut free from the evil by which it had been bound.

18. Bria, *Go forth in Peace,* 3, in Vassiliadis, "Reconciliation," 38.

rights almost always hides its true nature from its own self. It is by its very nature delusional: perpetrators of human rights violations redefine morality and start believing that they can commit systematic murder and other atrocities 'for the greater good.'"[19]

The Spirit of truth is able to reveal what is life destroying and what is life-giving, and where the church prefers the stifling idols of self-protection to the freedom of vulnerable self-offering love. Christians who are attentive to the Spirit of life will hear a warning wherever the grace and sovereignty of God are relativized, as when P. T. Botha stated, "The honor and duty to defend one's country shouldn't be made subservient to one's religious convictions."[20] Or when President Truman wrote after the bomb exploded over Hiroshima, "We thank God that it [the bomb] came to us . . . and we pray that he may guide us to use it in his ways and for his purposes."[21] When the Spirit came on Saul, he discovered he was violating the very God he hoped to serve by destroying followers of the Way. The Spirit was able both to turn Paul from that behavior and to fill him with love for his former enemies.

Vibrantly Diverse Communities United in Christ

Not only does the re-creative Spirit of life cut people free from that which binds them, the Spirit also pours out the creativity of diverse gifts and abilities on the one body of Christ. Even the outpouring of the Spirit at Pentecost reflects such unity in diversity. People were empowered to speak and understand one another across diverse languages and cultures. Thus, Kirsteen Kim suggests that the Holy Spirit should not be confined to images of a white dove only, but seen as a "multicolored reality" and multifaceted imagery that includes "breath of fire" and "overflowing water." Kim writes, "The dove seems to me hardly compatible with the raw power and vibrant colour of the Spirit, who brooded at the creation, inspired prophets, propelled the infant church into mission, transformed lives, and freed people from all kinds of bondage. In our imagery, we have captured the dove of freedom and power, and caged it. The heavenly dove has become like the doves in the temple that were being sold for sacrifice (Matt. 21:12–13)."[22]

19. Gobodo-Madikizela, *A Human Being Died*, 59.
20. Cited in ibid., 73.
21. Cited in Nouwen, *Road to Peace*, 13.
22. Kim, "The Reconciling Spirit," 21.

Thus, as mentioned previously, monolithic views of the new creation must give way to more vibrant and dynamic understandings that honor the pluralities included in the Spirit's creative work. In contrast to those mission efforts that treated all people as "sheep bound under paternal-ecclesial care," and that ignored "their intimately particular characteristics" of "tribal, linguistic, or geographic specifics," the new creation involves the reality of "all flesh" receiving the outpouring of the Holy Spirit.[23] The Spirit vivifies and anoints people in their physicality, which cannot be separated from their spirituality.[24] The Spirit is not disincarnate but is the animating force behind all of life. In the beginning this involved the creation of life itself. Since Pentecost it has meant a new creation, involving all flesh and without any expression of the kind of pigmentocracy that has at times been associated with Western theology and mission.[25]

Douglas Campbell in writing on Paul's letter to the Galatians (specifically 3:26–28) describes this new state as "a uniform, but personal and pluralized condition."[26] Colin Gunton summarizes this idea: "In other words, the oneness which Paul attributes to his readers is not asserted at the cost of personal particularity and difference. Overall, there is a change of place, achieved by and 'in' Christ which has ontological implications for the Church" and which constitutes a new eschatological state.[27] In describing the new creation, Paul maintains both his "other commitments to Jewish historical particularity and individual bodiliness" and the affirmation of "oneness of sonship (in the sense that all are now 'sons' in Christ)."[28]

Specifically in terms of reconciliation, this speaks to the call to "no longer see people as we once saw them," but now to see the supreme identity marker for all as being "in Christ" (2 Cor 5:16–17). Differences are no longer the means by which people are ranked, but provide the unique and pluriform ways through which the love of God is conveyed. Thus as Catherine LaCugna writes, "Human persons can be fully mutual, reciprocal,

23. Jennings, *Christian Imagination*, 27. See also Volf on the contrast between the totalizing nature of all "imperial projects" as reflected in Babel, and the affirmation of irreducible differences in Pentecost which evoke the image of "salutary harmony" in *Exclusion and Embrace*, 226–27.

24. For discussion of the integration of body, soul, and spirit see Brown et al., *Whatever Happened to the Soul?*

25. Jennings, *Christian Imagination*, 31–38.

26. Campbell, "Reconciliation in Paul," 45.

27. Gunton, "Introduction," 3.

28. Campbell, "Reconciliation in Paul," 45, n.16.

equal because we see in the proclamation and life of Jesus that the summit of personhood is to transcend (not escape from) every limit condition, including or especially gender, where gender means sex-role. In the reign of God human beings are judged on how they love others, not on whether they are male or female, white or black, bright or mediocre."[29] Rather than producing a process of assimilation and homogenization, the new creation initiates a symphonic process of ever-expanding harmonies that resonate with God's melodious will.

Vision and Imagination to Perceive God's Presence and Work in the World

The Holy Spirit's re-creation of God's people includes re-creation of our imaginations with new vision, new dreams, and new understanding. This is part of what it means to share in the divine nature (2 Pet 1:4) and to participate in the wonders of God's own imagination.[30] MacDonald viewed the Father and the Son as bonded together in love and overflowing by the Holy Spirit in love and creativity in the universe. Thus he affirmed the imagination as first and foremost an attribute of God, derivative of God's love.[31] "The imagination of man is made in the image of the imagination of God. . . . It will help much toward our understanding of the imagination and its functions in man if we first succeed in regarding aright the imagination of God, in which the imagination of man lives and moves and has its being."[32]

God's imagination has been linked specifically to the Holy Spirit, "let loose and working with all the freedom of God in the world, and in the lives, the words and actions, of the men and women of our time."[33] To share in God's imaginative creativity means to be rooted in divine love, meaning, and purpose, from which flow God's own imaginative initiative. "Divine

---

29. LaCugna, *God for Us,* 282. LaCugna offers one way of using Trinitarian understanding to warrant Christian ethical conclusions. Another way would be to develop Augustine's teaching (*On the Holy Trinity,* 400–416) in which the Holy Spirit is the bond of love between the Father and the Son, and the grace of God is identified as the love of God spread abroad in our hearts by the Holy Spirit.

30. For a more extensive discussion of God's imagination see Dearborn, *Baptized Imagination,* 77–82.

31. Ibid., 77.

32. MacDonald, "The Imagination," 6.

33. McIntyre, *Faith Theology and Imagination,* 64.

initiative is part of God's loving nature and thus it is wielded in creative self-giving."[34]

The Spirit gifts people of the new creation to envision life in harmony with God's life-giving and life-honoring ways. Ongoing dependency on the Spirit for God's visions and dreams is essential. As MacDonald clarified, the image of God in which humans are created includes their imaginative capacity, but that capacity is always derivative such that true creativity remains the purview of God, who alone can create *ex nihilo*.[35] Humans are creative by the power and love of the Holy Spirit at work within them, never in an autonomous fashion.[36]

If new creation is made possible by our having been grafted into Christ, then abiding in Christ is as essential for creative fruitfulness as a grapevine's attachment to its trunk is for juicy clusters of grapes. Paul affirms in a key passage on reconciliation that it is "in Christ" that we share in the new creation (2 Cor 5:17). To make our home in Christ, the true vine, is to recognize God's purpose to welcome all people and all of creation into this new home. As Wan writes, "It would be a mistake to understand 'new creation' in an individualistic sense" that would have been "foreign to the type of apocalyptic Jewish thinking from which Paul draws his imagery."[37] Rather, a vision of new creation includes the organic interconnectedness in Christ of all things whether in heaven or on earth (Col 1:20). To make our home in Christ, the true vine, is to recognize God's purpose to welcome all people into this home. That is the force behind reconciliation. Thus it was possible for Mandela and Martin Luther King Jr. to envision the interconnectedness in Christ of themselves even with their oppressors. It was the presence of the Spirit helping Peter to hear and believe that, "What God has made clean, you must not call profane" (Acts 10:15).

The difficulty of living by the Spirit in the new creation is that so many vestiges of the old creation remain. As Julian of Norwich conveyed, though

---

34. Dearborn, *Baptized Imagination*, 81.

35. The author acknowledges the significant debate in current theological circles on the viability of the idea of *creatio ex nihilo* in conveying the wonder of God's creation out of the abundance of God's triune love. It is beyond the purview of this book to address that debate here, but rather as previously mentioned I affirm with Kallistos Ware that *creatio ex nihilo* includes God creating all things out of self-giving love, but not out of preexistent materials.

36. For further reading on MacDonald's insights on the imagination see Dearborn, *Baptized Imagination*, 78ff.

37. Wan, *Power in Weakness*, 87.

we have been re-created, reborn through Jesus' labor pains on the cross, we are also invited into the process of growing as God's children into the full stature of his sons and daughters.[38] This requires being nurtured by his life, as children are nurtured by their mother. It also requires a vision for what God is doing to draw all things in heaven and on earth into God's reconciling love (Col 1:20). The new creation, which includes God's faithful renewal of the original creation, will ultimately only be fulfilled in "the life which is eternal."[39] As Moltmann writes, "We are still involved in the experience of renewal, and the becoming-new travels with us."[40] God is present in us by the Spirit, and "the goals of hope in our own lives, and what we ourselves expect of life, fuse with God's promises for a new creation of all things."[41] We turn now to that hope which is sustainable in the midst of the old creation, not because of the old orders' latent potential for new life, but because the author of life is bearing it through death into glorious newness.

Hope

The Holy Spirit offers a second pertinent gift of new hope, which also draws on and fuels the imagination as a resource for reconciliation. As Moltmann writes, "Believing hope will itself provide inexhaustible resources for the creative, inventive imagination of love."[42] The gift of hope flows directly from the Holy Spirit's gift of new creation in Christ. Paul prays that God's people will in fact "abound in hope by the power of the Holy Spirit" (Rom 15:13b). Fundamentally hope comes to us as an offering of God through the Holy Spirit in ways that reframe our entire way of conceiving and imagining our lives. No longer are we strangers and aliens, but rather we are adopted into Christ, a new community, a royal priesthood, God's own people.

This can sound like a lofty and unreachable ideal when contrasted with the fragmented and dehumanizing realities of our world. But the hope that the Spirit brings is integral to God's reconciling ways. First, this hope is substantial because it is hope in the living God, who made the heavens and

---

38. See Julian of Norwich, *Showings,* and Dearborn, "The Crucified Christ as the Motherly God."

39. Moltmann, *Spirit of Life,* 155.

40. Ibid.

41. Ibid.

42. Moltmann, *Theology of Hope,* 34.

the earth.[43] Second, it is comprehensive, for it is hope of the reconciliation of all things and all people to God and to one another, aligning with God's self-revealed will for shalom.[44] Third, it is empowering, fostering the conviction that change is possible through the power of God's Spirit to transform and to create one beloved community out of many tribes, tongues, and nations—or even out of fractured homes, families, and communities. Fourth, hope is not only empowering, it is essential for any movement toward change, and if it is to be substantial, derives from the costly process of confession and repentance.

Hope That Is Substantial

Hope for reconciliation is rooted in God, as both "the hope laid up for you in heaven" and a hope that inhabits God's people through the Holy Spirit: "Christ in you, the hope of glory" (Col 1:5, 7).[45] Thus, it can neither be reduced to an escapist otherworldly hope nor to a purely subjective feeling. So substantial is this hope that Bishop Desmond Tutu at one point described himself as a "prisoner of hope."[46] As Allan Boesak writes, "It is a hope often brutally crushed but which remains resilient because it receives its life from the God 'who executes justice for the oppressed' and who 'lifts up those who are bowed down' (Ps 146:7, 8)."[47] And because it is a hope in the Creator whose love extends to all, it creates a restlessness for all to know this hope. "For to this end we toil and struggle, because we have our hope set on the living God, who is the Savior of all people, especially of those who believe" (1 Tim 4:10). Paul describes the expansive nature of the hope of Christ's indwelling in relation to "being rooted and grounded in love," and comprehending "with all the saints, what is the breadth and length and height and depth, and to know the love of Christ that surpasses knowledge, so that you may be filled with all the fullness of God" (Eph 3:17–19).

43. Cf. 1 Pet 1:21: "Through him you have come to trust in God, who raised him from the dead and gave him glory, so that your faith and hope are set on God."

44. See Brueggemann, *Living Toward A Vision*.

45. See also Hebrews 6:19, where hope is "an utterly reliable anchor for our souls, fixed in the innermost shrine of heaven" (Phillips) and Acts 2:26, where Peter cites David's vision, "my flesh will live in hope."

46. Tutu, "BBC Breakfast with Frost," May 29, 2005.

47. Boesak and DeYoung, *Radical Reconciliation*, 143.

How does one access this infinite fullness of God's love and thus a hope in God? According to Paul, "God's love has been poured into our hearts through the Holy Spirit that has been given to us" and thus it a "hope [that] does not disappoint us" (Rom 5:5). To access this hope requires greater attentiveness to the presence and work of God in our hearts, a process more aligned with the work of the imagination than reason, as we will see in later chapters.

Hope That Is Comprehensive

Not only is the Holy Spirit's gift of hope one that is set on God, which includes being filled with all the fullness of God, it also has a specific direction and goal. The direction and goal are expressed in many ways but summed up in the New Testament as salvation, "*soteria*," which correlates to the Old Testament vision of shalom.[48] In many ways the loss of this Old Testament correlation of shalom with salvation has imperiled the very direction of the Western church, which has tended to prefer a more individualistic understanding of salvation and, as noted earlier, often ignored the communal thrust of the metanarrative of Scripture. This in turn has left room for the church to take the easy way of often dismissing the mandate to participate in God's ministry of justice and reconciliation. Christopher Wright contends that biblical hope is one that involves the larger social order and is the result of the outpouring of the Spirit: "The *social order* (Isa 32:17–18) will be restored to *shalom*. This beautiful word in Isaiah 32:17 speaks of human society enjoying the fruit of justice, which means the end of all violence, fear and dislocation because of the absence of all the things that produce them. In their place come rest, security, confidence and well-being. All this too the prophet sees as the result of the outpouring of the Spirit."[49]

Included in the comprehensive nature of this hope is the restoration of the entire created order. Human-centered notions of reconciliation have often created scenarios of escape from planet Earth rather than of its restoration and renewal. Contrary to our original mandate to tend and care

---

48. Cf. Snyder and Scandrett: "The great concern of the church is salvation and, biblically speaking, salvation ultimately means *creation healed*. . . . Of course, the gospel is also about justification by faith, atonement, forgiveness and new birth. But the larger truth that encompasses all of these is healing—complete healing, creation restored, true *shalom*." *Salvation Means Creation Healed*, xiv.

49. Wright, *Knowing the Holy Spirit*, 125.

for the garden, salvation has often been associated with its abandonment. But the hope of the gospel is that "the wolf shall live with the lamb, and the leopard shall lie down with the kid . . . for the earth shall be full of the knowledge of God as the waters cover the sea" (Isa 11:6a, 9b).

Hope That Is Empowering

Third, it is empowering hope because God not only wills the cosmic reconciliation of all things in Christ, but God is also present by the Spirit to make real transformation not only possible, but also inevitable. The oft-quoted phrase of Martin Luther King Jr. conveys this well: "The arc of the moral universe is long, but it bends toward justice," and according to Scripture, "reconciliation."[50] The seeds of this new-kingdom reality of justice and reconciliation were harrowed into the soil of humanity in the very flesh of Jesus Christ, who taught that the kingdom of God is both near and also to come. Images of the kingdom abound in Jesus' teaching, and include correlations with mustard seeds, yeast, the pearl of great price, hidden treasure, wedding feasts, vineyards, debt forgiveness, equal pay for all labor, and a fishing net with fish of every kind.[51] These are images of hiddenness, dynamism, joy, costliness, and radical change.

The hope of God's present and coming kingdom calls for radical engagement. Emmanuel Katongole writes, "I am a kingdom realist. The hope I want to point to is not out of this world, because the Word became flesh and made his dwelling among us (John 1:14). Jesus announced and established a new political order in this world and called it 'the kingdom of God.' It's not an ideal that we might achieve one fine day in the sweet by and by. God's kingdom is a reality into which Jesus invites us *now*."[52]

Hope as Essential and Costly

Hope is not merely part of the dynamic of change; change is obstructed without it. Even as a river requires open space to flow downhill lest it become a stagnant pool, human embrace of change requires the impetus and "broad place" of hope.[53] As Joseph Liechty writes, "People simply cannot choose

50. King Jr., "Where Do We Go From Here?"

51. See Matthew 5–21.

52. Katongole, *Mirror to the Church*, 110–11.

53. The psalmist uses the term "broad place" to indicate a place of rescue and

meaningful, uncoerced change without a certain level of confidence, and they will not change without trust and hope. Thus no reconciling process, whether personal or political, can go anywhere without these qualities."[54]

Changes needed for reconciling waters to flow happen when hope breaks through the dam of cynicism, hate, and fear, and when the waters flow forth between the banks of confession and repentance. Owning brokenness and active willingness to change are the means by which the transformation wrought by Christ may be experienced and enacted. The Holy Spirit brings awareness and conviction of sin as a wise guide leading people through turbulent waters. Confession liberates us from the back eddies of shame and guilt, to open us to the way of repentance. Though repentance is not a condition for forgiveness it is a consequence of fully receiving it.[55] And without repentance, reconciliation's healing waters will not be channeled into the very places where they are needed.

Liechty writes of the ways in which reconciliation attempts go wrong if justice and truth-seeking have been neglected or distorted. "For repenting this is obvious: it involves acknowledging and dealing with an injustice; repenting has no meaning outside the concept of justice."[56] He goes on to describe specific incidents where efforts to bring change and reconciliation have failed because of the lack of honest repentance. "The elusiveness of justice in Guatemala highlights the limitations of any reconciliation initiative when perpetrators remain unrepentant and unaccountable."[57] In situations like this, the imagination can play an immense role as will be developed shortly. Without a new vision, a transformed imagination, and the ability to see as if one were the "other," the deep repentance that is needed for ongoing hope and reconciliation becomes clogged. Rather than real hope taking people to new places, renewed cynicism grows like algae in this stagnant pool and hope in God for reconciliation is relegated to some otherworldly future, if kept at all.

In contrast, where hope of change and shalom are embraced as something God's people are called and empowered by the Holy Spirit to

---

hopefulness." See, for example, Pss 18:19; 31:8; 118:5.

54. Liechty, "Putting Forgiveness in its Place," 67.

55. "In short, what we have traditionally termed *repentance* should be interpreted as taking place not before forgiveness but after it—as stemming from the discovery of our prior unconditional forgiveness in the love of God." A. Torrance, "The Theological Grounds for Advocating Forgiveness," 55.

56. Liechty, "Putting Forgiveness in its Place," 66.

57. Ibid., 87.

demonstrate now, rivers of living water spring up and change does occur. An example can be seen in the Letter to Philemon, in which Paul is writing to a slave master with the hope of reconciling him to Onesimus, Philemon's slave. Max Turner describes Paul's hope, saying, "Paul evidently does expect a *radical transformation* of relationships. Philemon is implicitly invited to forgo his 'rights', and lovingly embrace Onesimus, *even* as he would Paul himself."[58] Paul, one of the more sectarian and rigid of Pharisees, has become an advocate for reconciliation across many great divides, including that of slave and master.[59] Paul's ability to draw people in from different ethnicities, faith backgrounds, and economic classes develops in part because he is so transparent about his own failures, based on his unflinching hope in the God who transforms and makes us new creatures in Christ.

In this way hope materializes, even if there is just a mustard seed of change at first. Jesus' pearl of great price becomes enticingly visible. The field of costly treasure becomes inviting for others. People are drawn in by the fragrance of bread that has not only risen from the new yeast, but has also been baked and broken for others. As Greg Jones writes, growth into the "self-giving love" of the Trinity in response to the costly forgiveness of Christ occurs "through the guidance of the Holy Spirit as Christians unlearn habits and patterns of domination and diminution of others, of sin and evil, and learn to embody habits and practices of Christian communion."[60]

Furthermore, the Spirit is also the one who empowers people to recognize the "high cost" of forgiveness, "both for God and for those who embody it," and to enter into "the disciplines of dying and rising with Christ, disciplines for which there are no shortcuts, no handy techniques to replace the risk and vulnerability of giving up possession of one's self."[61] Daily dying is a way of repenting, owning my/our brokenness, and lifting it from the shadows into the light.

Unfortunately, as Liechty notes, "the Western imagination is captivated by forgiveness in a way that repentance cannot match."[62] What does

---

58. Turner, "Human Reconciliation in the New Testament," 41.

59. Though Paul accommodates slavery in other texts like Colossians and Ephesians, he is clearly yeasting this new body of Christ with momentum toward just and harmonious relationships.

60. Jones, *Embodying Forgiveness*, xv.

61. Ibid., 5.

62. Liechty, "Putting Forgiveness in its Place," 60.

it take for the Holy Spirit to transform this predilection of the Western imagination for what Bonhoeffer called "cheap grace"?

Love

Reconciliation requires the third major gift of the Holy Spirit to be discussed in this chapter, and that is the gift of love. A participant in a conference hosted by Musalaha[63] made the following comment, "We are called by God to include each other, especially our 'enemies.' This was the radical message of the Messiah, 'Love your enemies and pray for those who persecute you' (Matt 5:44). Only through love can we direct our focus away from our own pain and see others through the eyes of the Savior. This does not excuse injustice, and where it is found it should be denounced and corrected, not through bitterness and hate, but through love."[64]

Sami Awad, a Christian Palestinian who leads an organization called Holy Land Trust in Bethlehem, trains people in nonviolent resistance to oppression, and in the healing and restoration of trust and relationships. In order to understand more fully his Israeli neighbors, Sami travels and takes others to Auschwitz to learn and to identify more fully with those who experienced the horrors of the Holocaust. It is not enough, says Sami, to resist oppression. Jesus calls us to love our neighbors and our enemies.[65]

Love is a difficult and even impossible human response to relation-shattering offences. The miracle of being able to love one's enemies is made possible by the Holy Spirit's presence, who would pour this love into our hearts (Rom 5:5). It is the cross of Christ that clarifies the nature of such love. Miroslav Volf describes three specific ways in which the cross enacts and reveals God's new covenant of reconciling love.

Love Is Making Space for Inclusion and Union

First, love involves profound union. "God renews the covenant by *making space* for humanity in God's very self."[66] This is not love as tolerance or distancing acceptance, but love as solidarity and inclusion, as expressed by the

63. An organization in Jerusalem founded to promote reconciliation between Palestinians and Israelis.

64. Musalaha staff letter, http://www.musalaha.org, June 17, 2010.

65. Decker and Medearis, *Tea with Hezbollah*, 186–220

66. Volf, "A Theology of Embrace," 27.

Musalaha participant above. Such love in social relationships would thus mean acknowledging that we are relationally constituted beings designed for community, not autonomy or isolation.

As Archbishop Desmond Tutu teaches, believers are like coal that will lose its heat and turn into a gray lump of cold ashes if separated from other believers.[67] Our identity includes the other(s), even those who have been enemies. This means being able to "transcend the perspective of our own side and take into account the complementary view of the other." It also means "attending to shifts in the other's identity, to make space for the changing other in ourselves and to be willing to renegotiate our own identity in interaction with those of others."[68]

Love Is Self-Sacrificing

Second, the cross points to love that is "*self-giving*."[69] God's covenant with humanity is restored because of the gift of God's own life in Christ, whose blood was shed for us. The covenant partner who was offended by the other's repeated covenant violations is the one who restores the covenant through self-sacrifice. Volf develops the implications of this for our reconciliation with one another:

> Partly because of the desire to shirk the responsibilities that accepting guilt involves, those who break a covenant do not or will not recognize that they have broken it. In a world of clashing perspectives and strenuous self-justifications, in a world of crumbling commitments and aggressive animosities, covenants are kept and renewed because those who, from their perspective, have not broken the covenant are willing to do the hard work of repairing it. Such work is self-sacrificial; something of the individual or communal self dies performing it. Yet the self by no means perishes, but is renewed as the truly communal self, fashioned in the image of the triune God who will not be without the other.[70]

67. Tutu, "My Search for God," in Battle, *Reconciliation*, 67.
68. Volf, "A Theology of Embrace," 28.
69. Ibid.
70. Ibid., 29.

Love Is Unconditional

Third, the cross reveals the unbound nature of love in the creation of an "*eternal*" covenant.[71] "Bound to Israel with 'bonds of love,' God cannot hand over Israel; God's commitment is irrevocable and God's covenant indestructible. Similarly, while a political covenant may be dissolved, a broader social covenant is strictly unconditional and therefore 'eternal'. It can be broken, but it cannot be undone."[72]

Volf goes on to describe the implications and radical nature of such a covenant of love. "Nobody is outside a social covenant, and no deed is imaginable that would put someone beyond its borders. The will to give ourselves to others and to welcome them, to readjust our identities to make space for them, comes before any judgement about them other than that of simply identifying them as human. The will to embrace precedes any truth about others, and any construction of our sense of justice. This will is absolutely indiscriminate and strictly immutable. It transcends our efforts to map good and evil onto our social world."[73]

Volf does not overlook the need for safety and justice for abused victims within this larger social covenant. This is not a description of insipid love that tolerates injustice, but of God's kind of love that ultimately loves unto purity, that transforms through its radical self-giving costliness. It is humanly impossible and thus utterly dependent on God's work in Christ on the cross and on the Holy Spirit's empowering presence in our lives and world. "Every generous act of giving, with every perfect gift, is from above, coming down from the Father of lights, with whom there is no variation or shadow due to change" (Jas 1:17). If the Spirit's work is to transform and enliven people to become more like Christ, the Spirit-given love expressed by God's people will resemble (even if only partially) Christ's love.

In light of such love, the kind of drivel that people often try to pass for love is exposed as a self-serving sham. Toni Morrison describes this sham of "love" in *Playing in the Dark*. One portrayal is of a well-educated and scientifically gifted Scot named William Dunbar, who became one of the eighteenth-century settlers in Mississippi. Dunbar wrote of the "Lord's commandment that mankind should 'love one another,'" and when the slaves he had brought from the Caribbean islands rebelled on his plantation

71. Ibid.
72. Ibid.
73. Ibid.

his response was, "Judge my surprise . . . Of what avail is kindness & good usage when rewarded by such ingratitude." His punishments were generally considered less severe than those of most slave owners. Yet when he recovered two runaway slaves, he "condemned them to receive 500 lashes each at five different times, and to carry a chain & log fixt to the ancle."[74]

Similarly, Willie Jennings describes the twisted antics some Western missionaries adopted to try to squeeze a justification of love out of the stone-hearted enslavement and conquest of indigenous peoples. One example cited is of Zurara, a Christian intellectual who was the royal chronicler for Prince Henry of Portugal in his conquest of Guinea, in West Africa. Zurara describes the agony and suffering of captured and auctioned Africans on August 8th, 1444. As he describes the misery of these people, he even remembers, "that they too are of the generation of the sons of Adam."[75] Yet he sees their suffering and their physical abuse as part of God's providential will and viable as a means of their salvation. He describes Prince Henry's noble aspirations as he tears family members from one another, "for of the . . . souls that fell to him . . . , he made a very speedy partition of these for his chief riches lay in his purpose; for he reflected with great pleasure upon the salvation of those souls that before were lost."[76]

Even Pope Nicholas V adopted this contorted way of thinking, or as Jennings describes it, this "imaginative framework." The Pope describes the conquerors as "athletes and intrepid champions of Christian faith." He continues, "Thence also many Guineamen and other negroes, taken by force, and some by barter of unprohibited articles, or by other lawful contracts of purchase, have been sent to the said kingdoms. A large number of these have been converted to the Catholic faith, and it is hoped by the help of divine mercy, that if such progress be continued with them, either those peoples will be converted to the faith or at least the souls of many of them will be gained for Christ."[77]

What went so wrong with Christian creativity, hope, and love that such inhumane treatment of others could be justified? Among the many things one could cite, one that will be discussed subsequently is a distorted moral imagination or a warped "imaginative framework" in which God

---

74. Bernard Bailyn, *Voyagers to the West*, 488–92, in Toni Morrison, *Playing in the Dark*, 43.

75. Zurara, *Chronicle of Guinea*, 80–81, in Jennings, *Christian Imagination*, 17.

76. Ibid., 19.

77. Jennings, *Christian Imagination*, 27.

was distanced and humans claimed God's place as the arbiters of human worth. The presence of the Holy Spirit, at work universally to draw people to God, was for all practical purposes denied, and the bridge-building gifts of the imagination were transformed into self-centered constructs that walled people out and kept them dehumanized.

4

The Holy Spirit's Work of Reconciliation
through the Imagination

Obedience follows imagination. Our obedience will not venture far beyond or
run risks beyond our imagined world. If we wish to have transformed obedience . . . then we must be summoned to an alternative imagination.[1]

What empowers people to live out lives of re-creation, hope, and
love that correspond with the truth they affirm and the Holy
Spirit that indwells them? What transforms approaches to
reconciliation from being empty verbal niceties or guilt-assuaging "quick
fixes" to dynamic expressions of the gospel? What is it that makes people
empathetic, caring, compassionate, forgiving, and ultimately loving toward
those who are "other"? This book has affirmed the reality that through the
Holy Spirit, God's love has flooded our hearts, uniting us with God and empowering us to participate in the reconciliation established by God through
Christ's life, death, and resurrection. Here we will explore the particular
roles the imagination plays in opening the heart's floodgates to both receive and release the Spirit's love to others. How can the imagination be
used to empower us to participate in day-to-day expressions of God's work
of reconciliation in Christ? What releases us to "breathe in the spirit that

1. Brueggemann, *Finally Comes the Poet*, 85.

delights in our being" and then "to breathe into the world this same spirit of delight"?[2]

Before responding to these questions, it's important to address a common assessment of the imagination that undermines its theological validity. In classes I teach on theology and the imagination, students often ask the question, "How can the imagination connect us with what is real (the object of theology), when the imagination concerns that which is fabricated and unreal (mythology)?" This frequent misperception has been so deeply embedded in the Western mind-set that reflection on the imagination has often been relegated to the salons of artists and poets and judged as unfit for those who focus on the "real"—scientists and theologians.

Much has been written on this in the past twenty years, and there is inadequate space to address this misperception here.[3] Suffice it to say that imagination has been embraced recently as a helpful tool of awakening and recovery, of taking people beyond the mundane experiences of life to places of deeper meaning and mystery. In *The Moral Imagination,* John Paul Lederach includes a description of the imagination inspired by George MacDonald's book *The Princess and the Goblin.* Imagination is a "power of perception, a light that illuminates the mystery that is hidden beneath a visible reality: it is the power to 'see' into the very nature of things."[4]

I propose three specific roles the imagination can serve in applying the gifts of the Holy Spirit toward transformation that are critical for participation in God's work of reconciliation. The first is as a solvent breaking down old, *in curvatus in se* ways of seeing the world in which I, my people, my nation are superior and more worthy than others.[5] This is the process of refining faith, sifting out the idols, and a response to Jesus' call, "Deny yourself." The second is in the imagination's creative facility to receive and offer a new vision of life, one that is *ex curvatus ex se.* Again, this is the process of renewing hope, reshaping one's vision of the object of hope, a response to Jesus' command, "Take up your cross." And the third is the integrative power of the imagination to connect the heart, mind, and body to

2. Boyle, *Tattoos on the Heart,* 151.

3. See, for example, authors like Walter Brueggemann, Paul Ricoeur, Janet Martin Soskice, John McIntire, and John Paul Lederach.

4. Guroian, *Tending a Heart of Virtue,* 141, in Lederach, *The Moral Imagination,* 27. For more on this see Dearborn, *Baptized Imagination,* 67–120.

5. A. Torrance, "The Theological Grounds," 50. I am indebted to James Fowler for his tripartite description of the work of the imagination as solvent, creative, and catalyzing in his "Future Christians and Church Education," 103–4.

this new vision, and to catalyze transformed responses. This is the process in which the Holy Spirit uses the imagination to enflame love in the new heart remade by Christ, and to empower one to respond to Jesus' call, "Follow me."[6] It is a process through which the Spirit's gifts of creativity, hope, and love can propel us forward in the life-giving waters of reconciliation.

We will explore the ways in which the imagination is a vital means by which the Holy Spirit's gifts of faith, hope, and love can bear fruit that tastes of the indwelling life of Jesus Christ. Again, this is not to say that the imagination is not also a tool that can be used to very damaging effects, as described powerfully by Willie James Jennings in *The Christian Imagination: Theology and Origins of Race*. More will be conveyed about such dangers in a forthcoming chapter. Yet even as Jennings describes the "spent orthodox imagination" of people like Colenso, and the inability of many missionaries to envision the Holy Spirit already at work in indigenous peoples, rather than just the devil ("demonic imagination"), he also argues for a "different imaginative modality" that harmonizes with God's purposes in Christ.[7] Distortions in the employment of the imagination do not warrant its marginalization, but reveal the powerful ways it can be deployed for good as well as for evil.[8]

The narrative of Peter and Cornelius in Acts 10 offers an illustration of the three dimensions of the Spirit's work through the imagination in breaking down barriers and fostering reconciled community.

Solvent

According to Paul, the relinquishment of old ways of seeing is integral to living out God's gift of reconciliation. "From now on, therefore, we regard no one from a human point of view" (2 Cor 5:16). The narrative of Peter and Cornelius demonstrates the Holy Spirit's harnessing of the imagination to break down a centuries-high separating wall that inhibited the spread of God's blessings through God's people to the nations.[9]

---

6. See Ezekiel 36:26 and Jeremiah 24:7, 32:39.

7. Jennings, *Christian Imagination*, 147, 98.

8. For a more extensive analysis of the imagination as a theological gift, including contrasts between a wise imagination and a bent imagination, and between reason and imagination, see Dearborn, *Baptized Imagination*, 89–94.

9. It is vital to note that Peter never relinquishes Jewish faith and practice but is invited to approach it in a transformed way.

Both Cornelius and Peter were in the habit of praying. Prayerful openness is one of the most crucial means by which one can receive God's transforming power to reshape one's imagination for participation in God's reconciling purposes. Nouwen speaks of the "urgency of prayer" as "the first characteristic of the work of peacemaking."[10] Learning to listen to God's voice and to be guided by God's loving Spirit is like placing oneself in the Potter's hands to be remolded and filled. It is difficult to create space for the other without having first created space in one's life for God through silent attentiveness. As Tutu writes, we need to quiet the "noisy demands of tribe and nation" to hear the voice of God that "speaks up on behalf of good. The practice of prayer attunes us to that voice."[11] Without this practice it is hard to make room for grace in our lives. In T. S. Eliot's words:

> Where shall the word be found, where will the word
> Resound? Not here, there is not enough silence
> . . . No place of grace for those who avoid the face
> No time to rejoice for those who walk among noise and deny the voice.[12]

Cornelius, a Roman centurion, is described as one "who gave alms generously to the people and prayed constantly to God" (Acts 10:2). Cornelius receives a vision of an angel of God "in dazzling clothes" who affirms Cornelius's faithfulness and calls him to send people to find Simon Peter (Acts 10:3, 30). Clearly God is with this "outsider" and through revelation is reshaping what he imagines possible, that God desires to shower grace on him, an uncircumcised Gentile, and on his family, and connect him in some mysterious way with Jews.

Peter, a Jewish follower of Jesus, is on the roof praying and also has his imagination infused with startling visions. These visions challenge the very roots of his religious understanding about what is pure and holy, and what is profane or unclean. Visions of "all kinds of four-footed creatures and reptiles and birds of the air" evoked a sense of revulsion in Peter, for the refusal to eat these creatures represented a fundamental distinction between Jews and Gentiles (Acts 10:12). His standards were under assault through the very fulfillment of the promise he had declared earlier—the promise that the Holy Spirit would bring new visions and dreams (Acts 2:17).

10. Nouwen, *Road to Peace*, 14.

11. Tutu, *Made for Goodness*, 176. Cf. Salter-McNeil: "We must learn to listen afresh to the voice of God—to ask God for direction and then to distinguish God's voice from the clamor of the culture and the crowds around us." *A Credible Witness*, 42.

12. Eliot, "Ash Wednesday," 65.

In fact, without this work of the Holy Spirit to offer a solvent to the old frameworks of his imagination, reconciliation with Cornelius would be unimaginable, because it would violate Peter's core identity. As Emmanuel Katongole expounds so well in *Mirror to the Church*, it is these very issues of core identity that divide people from one another and produce a "poverty of imagination."[13] The narrative in Acts 10 reveals that the reconciling work of the Holy Spirit takes Peter beyond merely dying to aspects of his personal identity. It calls him also to die to aspects of the corporate allegiances fueling his religious and ethnic imagination.

Peter's encounters with Jesus had already acted as a solvent on his personal identity. His false illusions about himself had been challenged in Jesus' presence many times. Peter had claimed an idealized sense of his own loyalty and courage that he was forced to relinquish again and again, in order to include weakness and dependency on Christ as integral to his self-understanding. As Tutu writes, "His newfound humility opened the space for God to use him."[14]

Yet Jesus' presence was also able to challenge Peter's self-understanding in his underestimation of himself. Even in Peter's first encounter with Jesus he is given a new name, "Peter," meaning "rock," and told he will be more than a fisherman. Though part of the uneducated working class, an outsider from Galilee, with an accent and appearance that gave him away,[15] he was included as an inner circle member of the Messiah's leadership team. Somehow he had to hold together his utter dependency on Christ, his tendency to sink on his own, with his new name and identity that transcended the branding of his regional, class, and vocational descriptors. As we will see, the ability to hold the tension of such contrasting ideas is itself a gift of the imagination.

In Acts 10, that which gave Peter meaning beyond his personal and contextual identity markers, being bound to a Jewish identity, also had to be relinquished to Christ and reshaped. Though he had already become the Lord's apostle, Peter still needed a fuller vision of himself and the nature of the Lord's mission that he would lead. One of the great gifts of the imagination is its ability to convey abstract concepts in concrete form. In this context, the Holy Spirit works through the imagination to give specificity to

13. Katongole, *Mirror to the Church*, 75.

14. Tutu, *Made for Goodness*, 119.

15. See Matthew 26:69–73.

the aspects of Peter's Jewish identity that needed denying.[16] So deeply embedded is this identity that transforming it requires three repeated visions of "defiling" creatures, and three times for the Spirit's clarification, "What God has called clean you must not call profane" (Acts 10:15–16). Peter did not become a non-Jew, but he began to relinquish that which made him feel superior to or more pure than non-Jews. Though still baffled by what the visions might mean, he was prepared by the Spirit to welcome Gentile messengers into his home, to be led by them to Cornelius's house, to share his food, and to embrace him and his family as a coheirs with Christ. Through God's visions and commands he came to see non-Jews very differently than he had before, no longer regarding them "from a human point of view." He could deny the things that, as a Jew, made him shun Gentiles. Neither Gentiles nor their food customs were profane. Having relinquished these very deep aspects of his identity, his faith shifted more fully from being centered in the things he should or should not do, to the God who makes clean and who offers a cleansed vision of the other.

Even as Jesus in the desert and on the cross denied the false identity offered to him by Satan, an identity of self-aggrandizement rather than of suffering, of power without love, so Peter is called to deny aspects of the identities to which he had been clinging. Jesus' call to self-denial is not just directed to the will, as has often been interpreted, but to the deeper core issues of identity that strain toward self-exaltation rather than solidarity with others. Peter's sense of who he is and whose he is requires a cleansing solvent before he can take up his cross and follow Jesus.

The ability to move us from self-preoccupation to an embrace of God's expansive love and compassion is one of the key gifts of the imagination fueled by the Holy Spirit. As Greg Boyle writes, "Compassion is always, at its most authentic, about a shift from the cramped world of self-preoccupation into a more expansive place of fellowship, true kinship."[17] Richard Rohr describes moving from the attempt to stand out to joyously sharing in the general dance.[18] Christian reconciliation, experiencing kinship with others, requires the ability to "imagine the expansive heart" of God.[19] As Nouwen

16. Cf. A. Torrance: "The Spirit of God is . . . there when the Spirit addresses [men and women] concretely in a manner which reforms and transforms their way of perceiving the world." "Accounts of the Spirit's Movement in Aotearoa/New Zealand," 77.

17. Boyle, *Tattoos on the Heart*, 77.

18. Rohr, *Falling Upward*, 120.

19. Boyle, *Tattoos on the Heart*, 27.

writes, "It is not so much a question of detachment as it is a question of fully trusting and following the voice of love. Detachment is only a consequence of a greater attachment."[20] Peter is able to detach from certain excluding aspects of his Jewish identity because Jesus has so completely attached himself to Peter in unconditional love. Perhaps the triple repetition of Peter's animal visions took him imaginatively back to Jesus' gracious and reconciling post-resurrection encounter with him on the shores of Galilee after his triple denial of Christ.[21]

Self-denial for the sake of the other is possible when we can grasp the immensity of God's love for ourselves and for all people. In this way the Holy Spirit may build a bridge to the other via the imagination's gift of new "sight" or seeing "as if," which becomes so evident in Peter's life.[22] The Holy Spirit uses the imagination's ability to "see as if" in two specific ways that are crucial to reconciliation. First, the Holy Spirit cleanses our imagination so we can view the other as a beloved child of God. As personal, social, and cultural identity markers are relativized through Spirit-led self-denial, the way is cleared for envisioning the deeper and more ultimate identity of the other. The other is no longer an "it" defined by class, race, gender, and ethnicity, but now is part of a common family, created in love by God, redeemed by Christ, and pursued by the Holy Spirit. We can begin to envision the other in David's terms, "As for the holy ones in the land, they are the noble, in whom is all my delight," because one has affirmed to the Lord, "You are my Lord; I have no good apart from you" (Ps 16:2, 3).

Second, we can begin to imagine life, even though partially, as if we were the other, this other whom the Spirit knows and loves and with whom the Spirit also dwells.[23] As Volf writes, to move into the world of the other, "We use imagination to see why their perspective about themselves, about us, and about our common history, can be so plausible to them whereas it

20. Nouwen, *Sabbatical Journey*, 173.

21. For an illuminating description of Jesus' restoring encounter with Peter and its relevance for the ministry of reconciliation, see Schreiter, *Ministry of Reconciliation*, 83–96.

22. For more on this subject see Dearborn, *Baptized Imagination*, 67–94.

23. This is not to say that there are no limits to empathy but that the imagination's ability to see some inner connection to the other is basic to honoring the humanity of the other. See, for example, Bennett, "The Limits of Empathy and the Global Politics of Belonging," 132–38. Greenberg summarizes: "Bennett examines the nature of empathy and identification: how the victim with a shared identity receives empathy while the alien body, such as the Afghan refugee or homeless person, is cast adrift." *Trauma at Home: After 9/11*, xxi.

is implausible, profoundly strange or even offensive to us."[24] Reconciliation depends on being able to move from encasing others in distancing categories to embracing them through community-enriched images. In fact, as Wendell Berry writes, for people to move into nonexploitive relationships with the other, "the only antidote . . . is imagination. . . . You have to be able to imagine lives that are not yours or the lives of your loved ones or the lives of your neighbors."[25] This leads us to the re-creative element of the imagination that is evident in the Holy Spirit's engagement with Peter and with all reconcilers.

Peter has received visions that dissolve some of the barriers between him and the other, deepen his faith in the God who cleanses all people, and open him to the possibility of seeing as if he were the other. The visions are a significant element in the variety of ways God employs to reshape Peter's imagination, including the Spirit's direct command, and as we will see, fulfilled predictions, memories of Jesus' ministry, and the Spirit's baptism. God's creativity through a lengthy process is needed to build bonds of kinship and unity with the other.

Creative

The imagination is not only a solvent that fosters healthy self-denial, but also a means by which the Holy Spirit creates bonds of kinship that both surmount and yet are enriched by differences. The Holy Spirit infuses the imagination with a new vision and new hope based in the cross of Christ. The new vision is not just of individual rescue, but also of a new creation and a new community. Thus, to "take up your cross" involves being bound with all those whom Jesus' cross includes. "God was in Christ reconciling the world to himself" (2 Cor 5:19). It is a willingness to suffer with Jesus, because of his identification both with the God who suffers and with all the "others" whom God loves.

This kind of cross bearing is evident in Peter's engagement with Cornelius in Acts 10. Peter has been called to deny himself by relinquishing traditions that separate him from his uncircumcised Gentile brother, Cornelius. Now he faces the demand for creativity, a new beginning in accordance with Jesus' call to him. He quickly learns that such new creation flows from a cruciform life that shares in the life of Jesus. To "take up his

24. Volf, *Exclusion and Embrace*, 252.
25. Wendell Berry, "Web Exclusive."

cross" connects him with the very creative identity of Jesus, in which life flows from death, fruitfulness from seeds buried in the ground, and new community from the soil of ancient enmity.

Even as Jesus had bound himself to sinners and enemies through his life and death, now Peter's repeated visions open him to a new possibility of being free to bind himself to one who normally fits the category of enemy, outsider, and oppressor. The "new creation" described by Paul in 2 Corinthians 5:17 emerges from this mutual self-binding. As Peter reflects on the vision, the Spirit tells him to welcome visitors, "for I have sent them" (Acts 10:19). To welcome them into his home would have been unthinkable prior to these visions and this command. Peter clarifies that engaging in such an intimate encounter with Gentiles as to share one's home and one's table ("to associate with or visit a Gentile") was considered "unlawful for a Jew" (Acts 10:28). To take up this cross is to embrace the God of the universe, who has welcomed him in all his brokenness along with these former outsiders. It takes an imaginative leap for Peter to move forward in this creative response. As Rita Guare writes, "Not only do prophets and poets discern the new actions of God, but also they institute these new actions by the power of their imaginations."[26]

John Perkins describes how difficult it is to enter into this creative process through which oppressive enemies become part of one's valued community. Lying in hospital, discouraged, and in pain from being unjustly beaten by white policemen, Perkins let his imagination roam through memories of defeats and setbacks in the struggle for racial justice. He describes becoming aware of the Holy Spirit: "The Spirit of God kept working on me and in me until I could say with Jesus, 'I forgive them, too.' . . . And he gave me the love I knew I would need to fulfill His command to me of 'love your enemy.'"[27] Perkins's key verse, Galatians 2:20, "I have been crucified with Christ . . . ," became operative in his life as the means through which by the Spirit he could approach former oppressors and enemies with the love of God.[28] According to Tutu, "When we forgive, we reclaim the power to create. We can create a new relationship with the person who has injured us."[29]

---

26. Guare, "Educating in the Ways of the Spirit," 78.

27. Perkins, *Let Justice Roll Down*, 195.

28. Ibid., 68.

29. Tutu, *Made for Goodness*, 150.

When the Spirit commands Peter "to go with them without hesitation; for I have sent them," Peter's immediate response is dramatic. He invites these Gentiles into his home, and gives them lodging. Eating together in Middle Eastern cultures expresses long-term commitment and loyalty, even oneness.[30] He takes the first step of welcoming the "other" into his home, and then the second step of accompanying these visitors to Cornelius's home in Caesarea. It is interesting that Peter is not told what he should do or say. His posture must be one of humble openness and responsiveness to what God is doing in these "others." There are no formulas, strategic plans, or well-beaten paths. Peter relies instead on the creativity of God. He travels with others to their context to hear what they have to say and what they desire of him, and to see what God will do.

Arriving at Cornelius's home, it would have been easy to revert to the old patterns of rejecting Gentiles as defiling pagans when Cornelius fell at his feet to worship him. How can such a response by Cornelius evidence the Spirit's cleansing work and preparation for the gospel? But Peter simply clarifies that he is mortal and enters in to see an entire group of people assembled to hear him speak. Seeing one another face to face is itself a significant part of the reconciliation process, as previously noted. Peter gives testimony to what God has just revealed to him and the dramatic challenge to his former way of thinking: "You yourselves know that it is unlawful for a Jew to associate with or to visit a Gentile; but *God has shown me that I should not call anyone profane or unclean*" (Acts 10:28, italics mine). He goes on to explain his new vision of God's re-creation, "I truly understand that God shows no partiality, but in every nation anyone who fears him and does what is right is acceptable to him. You know the message he sent to the people of Israel, preaching peace by Jesus Christ—he is Lord of all" (Acts 10:34).

The Spirit's revelation to Cornelius, through an angelic visitation and direction to find Peter, reflects God's active work among outsiders to include them in this family of new creation and new vision. This is not an arm's length encounter, but one that expresses the joy and intimacy of long-lost family members being reunited. We gain a glimpse in this of God's purposes, "God is bringing forth a whole new creation, redeemed by Christ and birthed by the Holy Spirit."[31] We encounter the wonder of the Holy Spirit as "the midwife of God's new creation" and the radical identity shift

30. See Acts 2:42–47.

31. Wright, *Knowing the Holy Spirit*, 33.

of being part of "God's new redeemed humanity."[32] Peter and Cornelius participate in and reflect the new creation of identities shaped by a new hope and new vision. Their identities are now *ex curvatus ex se*, because they share in the cruciform identity of Jesus Christ. Again, how is the imagination connected with this? No longer is their vision limited by fear of loss of cultural identity or even death. Their cleansed imaginations now offer a window to countercultural truths: life comes from death, new creation from the cross, and vibrant community from breaking down walls rather than constructing them.

Catalyzing

In addition to being a vehicle through which the Spirit cleansed aspects of Peter's identity that inhibited reconciliation with the other (solvent), and by which new connections with the other can be established (creative), the imagination serves the purpose of catalyzing powerful responses that ripple outward with explosive implications for the larger community. We see the dynamics of this in Acts 10 and 11, in Peter's own life, in his relationships with fellow believers, and with both seekers and skeptics.

This sequence of events begins with two people praying to God and quickly becomes two larger communities being joined together by the Holy Spirit. It becomes catalytic in part because both Peter and Cornelius are obediently responsive to the surprising visions they are given. They act on what they have seen and heard, rather than treating revelation as merely a set of new concepts to ponder. So confident are they that God has "spoken" to them, that both Peter and Cornelius quickly draw others in to share in their responses to God's specific commands. Peter takes "some of the believers with him" (Acts 10:23), which we later learn were "six brothers" (Acts 11:12). Cornelius "had called together his relatives and close friends" (Acts 10:24). When Peter and Cornelius meet, both share their experiences of the Holy Spirit's revelations to them, which are unique but also interlocking.

Peter also reflects active obedience in relating the gospel of Jesus' identity and ministry to this outsider to the faith.[33] He is authentic in his

---

32. Ibid., 34.

33. Volf writes, "As Hauerwas has argued, truth requires a *truthful life.* 'Our ability to "step back" from our deceptions is dependent on the dominant story, the master image, that we have embodied in our character' [Hauerwas, *Truthfulness and Tragedy,* 95]." Volf, *Exclusion and Embrace,* 255.

witness to Jesus, and not ashamed of the gospel, even though Cornelius, as a Roman military leader with sworn ultimate allegiance to Caesar, could have been quite offended. But Peter's authentic witness also honors Cornelius as having some knowledge of Jesus, rather than arrogantly assuming he is utterly clueless as a nonbeliever: "You know the message he sent to the people of Israel, preaching peace by Jesus Christ—he is Lord of all" (Acts 10:36). Peter honors Cornelius's existing knowledge, trusting that God has already been active with him. In this statement he both highlights the particular uniqueness of Israel, and the universal nature of Jesus' lordship. It's a powerful example of honoring the Holy Spirit's work in Cornelius's life but also seeking to draw him further into the unique revelation of God in Jesus Christ. Peter describes Jesus as the one who was anointed by God with the Holy Spirit, and "went about doing good and healing all who were oppressed by the devil, for God was with him" (Acts 10:38). He conveys how Jesus was put to death but raised by God on the third day and appeared to the disciples—even that he ate and drank with them. "He commanded us to preach to the people and to testify that he is the one ordained by God as judge of the living and the dead" (Acts 10:42).

Peter's imaginative scope has been stretched. He envisions Jesus as Lord of all people, such that all people need to hear about this one who is now the judge of the living and the dead. Peter's vision even extends to their inclusion in the gift of forgiveness of sins: "All the prophets testify about him that everyone who believes in him receives forgiveness of sins through his name" (Acts 10:43). But Peter's vision is stretched even further to see that in addition to forgiveness of sins, God desires to fill them with God's Spirit. "While Peter was still speaking, the Holy Spirit fell upon all who heard the word. The circumcised believers who had come with Peter were astonished that the gift of the Holy Spirit had been poured out even on the Gentiles, for they heard them speaking in tongues and extolling God" (Acts 10:44–6). For Peter it correlated with the way in which God acted to confirm Joel's "Day of the Lord" in Acts 2.

Now it is starkly evident to Peter that God desires these Gentiles to be completely grafted into the family of God. Peter is catalyzed to perform the great sacramental act of inclusion: baptism. "'Can anyone withhold the water for baptizing these people who have received the Holy Spirit just as we have?' So he ordered them to be baptized in the name of Jesus Christ. Then they invited him to stay for several days" (Acts 10:47-48).

This is clear evidence that the dividing walls have been brought down, and that reconciliation and unity are the gift of God in Christ and by the Holy Spirit. As De Gruchy writes, "If the first Pentecost was an outpouring of the Spirit on Jewish believers whether in Jerusalem or the *diaspora*, the second [Acts 10] attested to God's acceptance of people from every ethnic background and to God's will to incorporate them into a new community."[34] He goes on to describe baptism as the "basis of a new identity," that "should fundamentally change relationships within the community in a way that directly affects the structures of both Church and society."[35] In Acts, the church feels the initial shock waves of this new reality as far as Jerusalem.

So radically catalytic is this series of reconciling events that Peter must go up to Jerusalem to explain what has happened. Rather than being joyful and grateful for God's expansive love, "the circumcised believers criticized him, saying, 'Why did you go to uncircumcised men and eat with them?'" (Acts 11:2, 3). Their expectations have been framed by imaginations that have yet to be fully cleansed and re-created by God's Spirit. Transformation occurs, however, not by receiving visions of their own, but through participating vicariously in these experiences as Peter shares a detailed narrative of what occurred. Narrative is shown to be yet another way that the imagination can be used by God's Spirit to offer a solvent, new creation, and catalytic transformation for the purposes of reconciliation.

As evident with Peter, reconciliation is a demanding process. Peter was sent to Caesarea to be with the Gentiles to participate in God's work of drawing them in, and now to Jerusalem to explain to the Jews why Gentiles also belong. It's not clear which was the more difficult journey. Leaders who have been active in ministries of reconciliation often have a difficult time convincing their own constituencies of the depth of the kinship and bond that now exists with those formerly considered outsiders.[36] John Perkins describes deep anguish in a white pastor whom he befriended, and who ultimately befriended him. So disturbed was this pastor by his congregation's stubborn resistance to his work with a black minister that he gave up and committed suicide.[37]

34. De Gruchy, *Reconciliation*, 83–84.

35. Ibid., 97, 99.

36. See, for example, the resistance among their own communities to people like Bartolomé de Las Casas and Hudson Taylor, who challenged dehumanizing views of non-Europeans and advocated greater solidarity with them.

37. Marsh and Perkins, *Welcoming Justice*, 36.

Though the Jewish believers had received no revelatory vision that we know of regarding what Peter had been doing to prepare them for his testimony of God's faithful inclusive love, they are transformed by the gift of the Spirit working through their own imaginations. First, the power of the narrative of these visions and experiences is compelling and authenticating. Second, Peter is able to bridge these foreign experiences and images to their own imaginations through reminding them of words they had heard Jesus speak and their own anointing by the Spirit. "And I remembered the word of the Lord, how he had said, 'John baptized with water, but you will be baptized with the Holy Spirit.' If then God gave them the same gift that he gave us when we believed in the Lord Jesus Christ, who was I that I could hinder God" (Acts 11:17)?

Peter conveys the shocking news to them in ways that touch their hearts, minds, and imaginations. He does not rely on theological disputation, but draws them into his own narrative, showing how it fits within the larger faith narrative and Jesus' specific teaching, asking pertinent questions and leaving them to draw their own conclusions. In this way it catalyzes their praise of God and willingness to accept a radical paradigm shift. "When they heard this, they were silenced. And they praised God, saying, 'Then God has given even to the Gentiles the repentance that leads to life'" (Acts 11:18).

Reconciliation requires visionaries like Peter, who are open to God's wisdom and ways—people who prayerfully receive the cleansing, re-creative, and catalyzing presence of the Holy Spirit to transform their imaginations. As we have discussed, this means they are willing to deny themselves, take up their cross, and follow Jesus. In this way they become participants in Jesus' vicarious work on our behalf to reconcile us to God and to one another. As De Gruchy writes, "It is through the mediation of human beings, fallen and fallible, but also seeking to be a community of vicarious love in the world, that reconciliation becomes a reality."[38]

Such leaders are able, like Peter, to "retrieve the notion of covenant from the narrow and exclusive way in which it has been used, and restore its inclusive meaning and the moral commitments that it demands."[39] For the circumcised believers in Judea the meaning of covenant has begun to change radically in ways that challenge them to imagine God, their own

---

38. De Gruchy, *Reconciliation*, 95.

39. Ibid., 183.

identity, and the future of the church differently.[40] Covenant evokes images that connect with God's universal concern for all people and with the kingdom of God as described in Revelation 7:9, people from every tribe, tongue, and nation, rather than remaining a world that mirrors back only people like "me."

---

40. The challenging nature of this reimagining process is evident in the need for two other councils (Acts 15, 21) to deal with related barriers. Peter's transformation in accepting nonkosher people with faith in Jesus Christ was not convincing to some in the Jewish church. It is important to acknowledge that transformation takes different stimuli, forms, and processes, though the aim of this book is to highlight the work of the Spirit through the imagination.

5

The Imagination's Third Way

Because in Him the flesh is united to the Word without magical
transformation,
Imagination is redeemed from promiscuous fornication
with her own images . . .
Because in Him the Word is united to the Flesh without loss of perfection,
Reason is redeemed from incestuous fixation on her own Logic,
for the One and the Many are simultaneously revealed as real.[1]

I f the imagination is a gift from God and can catalyze such change, why
has it often been ignored as a resource for participation in God's kingdom work? What specific qualities of the imagination make it such a
powerful tool for the Holy Spirit's work of transformation and reconciliation? What further role does the imagination play in helping to create a
new community in which there is "neither Jew nor Gentile, slave nor free,
male and female," and yet where those distinctions are still honored as a
place from which particular gifts and perspectives can be offered?

David Brooks writes that for too long Western societies' character-
building models have emphasized will and reason as the prime factors in
decision making. Much effort has been applied to train people in the critical and informed use of reason, and significant training has been exerted to

1. Auden, *For the Time Being*, 50, 52.

strengthen the will. But little emphasis has been applied to rightly shaping perception. Brooks writes, "Both reason and will are obviously important in making moral decisions and exercising self-control. But neither of these character models has proven very effective. . . . Most diets fail because the conscious forces of reason and will are simply not powerful enough to consistently subdue unconscious urges."[2] Unconscious urges and perceptions are accessed and shaped through the imagination. Perceptions may be encoded differently by training and using one's imagination.[3] He argues that it is time to take the imagination more seriously in terms of the perceptions we have and the responses we make.

Brooks uses the example of Erica, a girl from a dysfunctional background who learns to reframe the way in which she perceives reality for more positive and life-giving outcomes. He describes it as a "learning-to-see model" that is powerfully influenced by community and the discipline of regular "small and repetitive action."[4] Central to the process of transformation for Erica was applying her imagination toward a more positive way of perceiving herself and the world.[5]

Biblically, Saul of Tarsus (ultimately referred to as Paul) provides an example of such transformed perception through the vehicle of the imagination. His life was zealously committed to serving God and the people of God through a particular imaginative construct shaped in him by his community, his study of the Torah, and the disciplines involved in being a Pharisee. Simply put, in this construct God was for the Jews, and the people who challenged Jewish faith were to be destroyed by faithful followers of God. Saul took the need for their destruction so seriously that he watched as Stephen was stoned to death and journeyed to places where he could round up and destroy followers of Jesus. He was a zealot fighting for a particular framing of God's nature and will that would bless the few and condemn the many.

So radically does he learn to see differently that he becomes the author of one of the greatest descriptions of love ever written (1 Cor 13) and an apologist for a view of God who sacrifices everything that all may be blessed: "For God has imprisoned all in disobedience so that he may be merciful to all" (Rom 11:32). Paul's vision of God is transformed to the

2. Brooks, *Social Animal*, 125–26.

3. Ibid., 125.

4. Ibid., 128.

5. Ibid., 131.

point of affirming that "through Christ God was pleased to reconcile to himself all things whether on earth or in heaven" (Col 1:20). What created such a radical change in Paul's perception that he would now be willing to lay down his life for the very people he formerly wanted to kill? What has made him, in his own words, a "new creation" who no longer "regard[ed] anyone from a human point of view" (2 Cor 5:16)?

Like Peter, Paul is given through the Holy Spirit a transformative vision. Paul's vision is of the very one who was at the heart of his battle, the object of his hatred and destruction, the one he held responsible for polluting orthodox faith. It was of Jesus. In his encounter with Jesus, he goes through the three-part process described in the last chapter. Again, the Holy Spirit first uses the imagination as a solvent to dissolve his false notions of God, of Christ, and of Christ's followers. "Something like scales fell from his eyes, and his sight was restored" (Acts 9:18). Somehow his perception is radically transformed, and it is his reason and will that follow closely behind, rather than leading the way. Thus he no longer knows Christ "from a human point of view" (2 Cor 5:16). The frameworks that had shaped his understanding of those who were elect and those who were nonelect have also been transfigured (see Romans 9–11).

Second, the Holy Spirit works through the imagination to create a new vision and a new understanding. Jesus becomes the unifying center of Paul's life and his faith. The framework of insiders versus outsiders has capitulated to a paradigm of Christ at the head of all things, drawing all things into harmony with God. This is a new imaginative framework for Paul's perception of all of life. So the very ideas he had opposed in the following of Jesus now become his own ideas and arguments, and he works to reshape his entire understanding of the Torah to fit within this new perception. Paul now argues for God as the savior of all people, as one with the Son of God, Jesus Christ, and as bound to the very people he had been persecuting.

Third, the Holy Spirit used the death of his former perception and the new creation of his redeemed sight to catalyze him into radical new action. "Immediately he began to proclaim Jesus in the synagogues, saying, 'He is the Son of God'" (Acts 9:20). So radical is the transformation in Paul that "All who heard him were amazed" (Acts 9:21), and "Saul became increasingly more powerful and confounded the Jews who lived in Damascus by proving that Jesus was the Messiah" (Acts 9:22).

What is it about the imagination that makes it a vehicle for the Holy Spirit's penetration into an extremely polarized situation to transform one of the most polarizing leaders into someone who refuses to adhere to either the Jewish or the Gentile "pole," but rather who is committed to arguing, living, and even dying for both Jew and Gentile?

Levison describes being filled with the Spirit as a way to move from fearfulness to embracing approaches of others.[6] Fundamental to that shift is relinquishing imaginative frameworks that exclude and that categorize people as the other, the alien, and the unacceptable. What happens when one's sight is raised up to envision reality beyond the usual categories? The imagination is able to take us into the realm of mystery and wonder, into aspects of reality that are beyond our categories and control. Pride and self-assurance give way to humility and awe. Eyes are opened to "fear in a handful of dust."[7] As Eliot affirms, "The only wisdom we can hope to acquire/ Is the wisdom of humility: humility is endless."[8]

A Powerful Bridge

Our hope lies . . . in the wisdom wherein we live and move and have our being. Thence we hope for endless forms of beauty informed of truth.[9]

Immense imaginative creativity from the Holy Spirit is needed to move Peter, Paul, and the early church beyond categorical thought forms that either divide according to differences or seek the complete dissolution of differences through assimilation. This is the imagination's gift of a third way. No longer are there only two options, either we are one and the same, or we are different and divided. In order to describe a third way between dualistic frameworks, Coleridge developed his theory of "polarity," which relies on both the Holy Spirit and the imagination. According to Coleridge, the dynamic relationship between two poles implies the presence of "a third something," which he described as "an interpenetration of the counteracting powers, partaking of both."[10] He used the word *co-inherence* to describe the interpenetration, or the differentiated unity.[11] For Coleridge

6. Levison, *Filled with the Spirit*, 277.

7. Eliot, "The Waste Land," 38.

8. Eliot, "Four Quartets," 126.

9. MacDonald, "The Imagination," 25.

10. Coleridge, *Biographia Literaria*, 310.

11. Coleridge, *Aids to Reflection*, 157. Corapi writes, "Coinherence is a favorite word

this threefold nature of reality led him to affirm belief in the Trinity as "the one substantive truth, which is the form, manner, and involvement of all truths."[12]

Viewed from a Trinitarian perspective, differing realities do not necessarily oppose, negate, or absorb each other, or stand in logical abstraction as in the case of paradox. Rather they may enhance each other and the dynamic between them then becomes a third reality—a bridge of interrelationship and interdependence. Polarity allows for distinctiveness without separation, and for unity in diversity.[13]

Marital relationships provide an illustration of both polarity at its best, and the dangers of a loss of this coinherence dynamic. A romantic relationship can begin with such a strong magnetic attraction that there is an obsessive desire by each to so strongly attract and draw the other in that it can be consuming. Language emerges at first that expresses a yearning to consume and absorb the other and to be absorbed into the other's life. As a healthy relationship matures, the individuals grow both in their own unique ways and yet also together, with the dynamic between them continuing to challenge and enrich both. In an immature relationship the challenge and tension of the polarity becomes a threat, and one dominant partner with one compliant partner can force such assimilation that the very magnetism that drew them together becomes absorbed into the self-aggrandizement of one of the parties. The traditional joke becomes no joke at all: "When in marriage the two become one, the question is, which one?" On the other hand, two dominant partners can adopt such parallel lives, devoting more time to their individual self-expression than to the relationship and to each other, that the magnetism between them also fades away. Differences that once drew them together now merely divide them. The challenges of honoring and learning from those differences are treated as too costly to have to cope with. This is especially problematic in a society that takes its imaginative framework of what it means to be human from individualistic and nonrelational models.

Coleridge reclaimed polarity and coinherence as fundamental to the nature of the triune God, and to the nature of reality created by God. God's nature as mutual indwelling persons, whose being is in communion,

---

of Coleridge's (the Latin translation of perichoresis) that signifies a differentiated unity." "History and Trinitarian Thought," 87.

12. Coleridge, "Note to *Confessions*," 86. Cf. Barfield, "Either : Or," 31.

13. Dearborn, *Baptized Imagination*, 31.

creates the foundational truth of all being and identity. Even as the Spirit can be seen as the bond of love between the Father and the Son,[14] sustaining difference and unity, the imagination can offer a bridge by which the Spirit unites people together in mutual understanding, love, and empathy. The Spirit through the imagination has the power to bridge disparate entities together in an ongoing tensive relationship that honors both like and unlikeness, while also enriching each of the polar entities.[15]

The Holy Spirit uses the imagination as a vital bridge of polarity also to cleanse and shape imaginative understanding of God and creation.[16] James Fowler describes the imagination as *"the principal human organ for knowing and responding to disclosures of transcendent Truth."*[17] The coinherence of the eternal in the temporal, the Holy Spirit as God's presence with us, makes possible the truth-bearing nature of the imagination, which through inspiration unveils the "hidden meaning" of creation and maintains the tension between the eternal and the temporal.[18]

Polarity is also evident in the imagination's gift of "bi-focality," in which the imagination is able to sustain a vision of two different entities at once as well as a relational bridge uniting them. This can be seen most simply in imagination's offspring, the analogy, which upholds a dynamic relationship of both "like and unlike" in two different entities. Such an analogy is evident in Jesus' command: "As I have loved you, so you must love one another" (John 13:34). There is a likeness and an unlikeness between Jesus and his disciples, and between Jesus' love and the disciples' love. The difference is not dissolved away in this analogy but becomes a means of enrichment, mutual participation, and coinherence. The life and love of Jesus frees us to be both more fully ourselves and more truly like him. The tension of the ongoing reality of difference will remain, yet as a dynamic force of vitality and unity. It is no wonder that analogical language is the language of theology. But what does this have to do with reconciliation?

The Holy Spirit is the creative source of new beginnings, of a third way that miraculously creates a bridge between polar realities and seemingly antithetical entities, like Peter and Cornelius, and Saul and the followers of

---

14. Augustine, *On the Trinity*, XV.v.7, 100; XV.xvii.27, 215; XV.xix.37, 219.

15. See Dearborn, *Baptized Imagination*, 30–34, 84–85, for more on the concept of polarity.

16. McIntyre, *Shape of Pneumatology*, 271.

17. Fowler, "Future Christians and Church Education," 104. Emphasis added.

18. Coleridge, *Aids to Reflection*, 120.

Jesus. The Spirit also inspires the imagination to be a vehicle through which a bridge is perceived and practiced, to enable people to hear God's voice and to move with the Spirit across that bridge. Thus even as one is enabled to imagine the other in a new way, as both the "other" and a beloved child of God, one is given a sense of coinherence with that other. Peter and Cornelius belong together in some mysterious way, without Peter becoming a Gentile or Cornelius becoming a Jew. Paul and the followers of Jesus were bound together in ways that the Gentile followers of Jesus could benefit from and be shaped immensely by Paul's Jewishness, and they in turn could give Paul a fresh vision of the lavish and liberating love of God. Even so, they are invited to live out their cultural and ethnic identities in new ways. Those identities became less constrictive and more porous, transformed in the very dynamic of being united in Christ. The bond of the Holy Spirit through the imagination allows for great freedom in the midst of deepened and broadened identities.

The Holy Spirit empowers the imagination to hold the tension that honors distinctiveness at the same time as shared identity. The new creation does not become a homogenized assimilation that denies former realities, but actually is a community all the more glorious because the former realities are harmonized and enhanced rather than denied or allowed to remain dissonant barriers. Peter's Jewish identity is no longer about remaining ritually pure but now draws on the deeper wells of his identity as a child of Abraham, called to be a vehicle of blessing for all people. Cornelius's Roman identity is no longer about dominance and rule but about submitting to one who is the supreme Lord of all, via God's lowly Jewish messenger. Sadly, however, as Rohr writes, "Organized religion has not been known for its inclusiveness or for being very comfortable with diversity. Yet pluriformity, multiplicity, and diversity is the only world there is!"[19]

The imagination accommodates growth in identity because of the way in which it includes mystery and dynamic change, and resists rigid barriers. It helps to empower people to move out of the "bipartisan divide" and into the "tripartisan" nature of mature elders.[20] The very either/or categories we tend to erect are often defeated by a creative vision of a third alternative that affirms both polar realities along with a transforming and enhancing

19. Rohr, *Falling Upward*, 60.
20. Ibid., 40.

relationship between them.[21] The imagination serves this function in multiple ways in the work of reconciliation.

A Healing Bridge Between Past and Present

For true reconciliation to occur, the imagination must sustain bi-focality and polarity in at least three areas for the creation of reconciled relationships. First, a transformative and imaginative bridge is needed between the past and the present. While moving forward in the present to resolve animosities, the imagination is needed to hold in tension the memory of past injustices and the hope of present healing. Emmanuel Katongole warns of the "danger of reconciliation without memory—the temptation to forget the wounds of history" and the tendency to "move too quickly to solutions that only mask our brokenness."[22]

The work of the Holy Spirit to help one both remember and forgive involves the imagination in profound ways. As flashbacks of painful past experiences strike yet coinhere with a desire for present forgiveness, a healing bridge may be built by which forgiveness can wash over those memories but not violate them by removing or denying them. "Forgiveness is not a form of forgetting. It is rather, a profound form of remembering. When we forgive, we remember who and whose we are. We remember that we are creative beings modeled on a creative God."[23] The horrors of the past impact the present desire for forgiveness, making it all the more pressing and urgent, while also clarifying the immense cost of such forgiveness.

For the perpetrator such an interface of remembrance and the gift of forgiveness can lead to a commitment to take on the burden of reparative action: to own their need to "remember and change," rather than leaving the victim with all the work, falsely seen as "forgiving and forgetting."[24] Imaginative polarity includes suffering and does not deny it. As Stephen Prickett writes in commenting on Coleridge's ideas about polarity, "Tragedy is a perpetual possibility; as the crucifixion reminds us, there is no easy reconciliation."[25]

21. This is not to say that all either/or categories are wrong or unhelpful. For further insight on this see Lewis, "Preface," *Great Divorce*, i–ix.

22. Katongole and Rice, *Reconciling All Things*, 82, 83.

23. Tutu, *Made for Goodness*, 150.

24. Lederach, *Moral Imagination*, 62.

25. Prickett, *Victorian Fantasy*, 187.

A Healing Bridge Between Fractured Relationships and Oneness in Christ

Second, bi-focality and polarity are needed to bridge the gap between the fact of relational alienation and the deeper truth of communion. For example, the reconciliation of racially divided groups necessitates honesty about racism as an ongoing structural and interpersonal reality, along with the truth of our common humanity. Harsh realities are not ignored but neither are they allowed determinative power to define relationships. As Lederach writes, "The moral imagination requires the capacity to imagine ourselves in a web of relationships that includes our enemies."[26] The tension remains; the fragmenting realities still exist and are not dissolved away in the process of reconciliation work. Yet these divisions are no longer determinative. They are relativized under the more ultimate reality of Christ having made us one, and now with the presence of the Holy Spirit nurturing that new life into existence. An inspired imagination perceives the "already" and "not yet" nature of our life together and refuses to default to either despair at the ongoing realities of brokenness, or escape the present pain by withdrawing into an idealistic or individualistic hope of healing.

A Bridge Between Present Brokenness and the In-Breaking Future of God

Third, the hope that is created by the Holy Spirit fueling one's imagination is a hope that also holds together that which has been, and the kingdom of God which is both present and yet to come in even fuller measure. As Wirzba writes, "Hope makes it possible for us to sing and rejoice even in the midst of our pain, because hope opens our being and our imagination."[27] The Spirit of God grants perception of both the concrete reality of our circumstances and insight into God's presence and action beyond what is obvious through our five senses. Thus, though Elisha's servant was terrified seeing the Aramean enemies that surrounded them, "Elisha replied, 'Do not be afraid, for there are more with us than there are with them.' Then Elisha prayed: 'O LORD, please open his eyes that he may see.' So the LORD opened the eyes of the servant, and he saw; the mountain was full of horses and chariots of fire all around Elisha" (2 Kgs 6:16–17).

26. Lederach, *Moral Imagination*, 5.
27. Wirzba, *Living the Sabbath*, 88.

Moltmann calls the ability to see both present brokenness and God's in-breaking future the "*novum.*"[28] The Holy Spirit partners with the imaginative gift of relational thought (polarity) that we might embrace both the great good coming and the real pain present, both the hope of all things being reconciled in Christ (Col. 1:20) with that which now separates us, both God's infinite goodness and our finite weakness.[29] As Tutu writes, "When we reconcile, we inhabit that territory conceived by the hope-filled imagination."[30] It is a vision that extends back to a "time before time," Tutu continues, "when all creation lived in harmony with God in the garden of Eden," and forward to the eschaton when people from every nation, tongue, and tribe will stream toward the Lamb (Rev 7:9).[31]

The imagination is the Holy Spirit's gift by which one can continue to live with these tensions and allow them to bear creative fruit. Furthermore the Holy Spirit is actively present breaking down barriers and wooing the creation into the "salutary harmony" for which it was created.[32] As Volf writes, "The Babylonian ascending movement of piercing the heavens that pulls up everything into a centralized homogeneity has given way to the Pentecostal descending movement of 'pouring' [Acts 1:17] from the heavens, which like rain, enables each of the 'varied living beings to burst into new life.' The tower at the center that outwardly controls the whole circumference is replaced by the Spirit that 'fills all' by 'descending upon each' [Acts 1:3]."[33]

For reconciliation to happen in a sustainable way, we must reimagine both ourselves and others in light of the reality that "God dwells in each of us. God dwells in each of us even when we are unaware of it."[34] As Tutu writes, "Accepting God's acceptance is what allows us to live out of our

---

28. Moltmann seeks to "link the eschatological category of *novum* with the anamnetic category of repetition in such a way that the beginning is gathered up into the end, and the consummation brings back everything that had ever been before." Moltmann, *Coming of God,* 265.

29. This hope is very different than that described critically by C. S. Song: "Most Christians are happy and contented as long as churches are overflowing with worshippers on Sunday, singing and praying in forgetfulness of the outside world." "Telling Stories of the Spirit's Movement in Asia," 2–3

30. Tutu, *Made for Goodness,* 153.

31. Ibid.

32. Volf, *Exclusion and Embrace,* 227.

33. Welker, *God the Spirit* (127), referenced in Volf, *Exclusion and Embrace,* 227–28.

34. Tutu, *Made for Goodness,* 193.

own godliness. It is what helps us to live into our own goodness."[35] And confidence that God is with us to sustain and provide for all of us is vital for imagining others no longer as a competitive threat but as "linked in the chain of our common humanity."[36]

A Higher Vista

The transrational has the capacity to keep us inside an open system and a larger horizon so that the soul, the heart, and the mind do not close down inside of small and constricted space. The merely rational mind is invariably dualistic.[37]

It takes lots of drowning in your own too tiny river to get to this big and good place.[38]

For George MacDonald, the imagination serves as a keen-eyed Pegasus that soars above the world to guide the packhorse of reason as it plods below. The imagination isn't abstracted from the world but is able to reveal a larger vision and to offer more holistic perspectives on the complexities and multivalent nature of reality. "The imagination 'sweeps across the borders, searching out new lands into which she may guide her plodding brother.' The imagination's discoveries were more important, 'only, wherever Pegasus has shown the way through a bog, the pack-horse which followed has got the praise of the discovery.'"[39] One can imagine the horse of reason trying to find its way through the maze of the many categories it has created to explain a given situation. Paul could give numerous rationales of why his persecution of the church made sense to him through the categories of election, chosen people, God of Abraham, etc. It wasn't until Jesus took him out of that maze through a vision that he could gain perspective on what he was doing, and on a God beyond all categories whose loving intentions extended to all.

35. Ibid., 182.

36. Ibid., 193.

37. Rohr, *Falling Upward*, xxxi.

38. Ibid., 113.

39. Dearborn, *Baptized Imagination,* 92–93, quoting MacDonald, "Imagination," 14; *Castle Warwick*, 46.

Similarly, John McIntyre describes the work of the Holy Spirit through the imagination as facilitating a larger perspective on Scripture. "It is the Spirit's use of imagination which lifts it beyond a two-dimensional reading of the history in Scripture to the grasping of the spiritual realities which are of the essence of Scripture."[40]

MacDonald also conveyed the imagination's ability to offer this expanded view in his use of the metaphor of the architect. "What we mean to insist upon is, that in finding out the works of God, the Intellect must labour, workman-like, under the direction of the architect, Imagination."[41] He viewed images as prior to concepts, and the imagination as that which could reach the heart. The prophetic or baptized imagination acts as an architect because through the heart it opens the door to understanding and to the meaning of all that God has created.[42]

The Holy Spirit uses the imagination to bridge divisions and reveal integral relationships between all things. The Spirit lifts us up on eagle's wings to show us the kingdom of God in our midst, and to guide us onto the paths of peace. One of the central ways this is accomplished is through sustained vision of Christ—the bridge and the rock that is higher than we. Jesus taught that the Spirit would "teach you everything, and remind you of all that I have said to you" (John 14:26). And Jesus pledges his peace, "Peace I leave with you; my peace I give to you" (John 14:27). Jesus' way is the way of peace in which we deny ourselves, take up our cross, and follow him.

Unless we are open to the Spirit and follow in Jesus' way, our efforts at reconciliation will not take us far out of the mazes of our own categories and narrow ideologies. Unless we are open to God's presence with us in the wilderness of fractured relationships, we will miss the Spirit's living water that flows even in the desert, and the multiplication of loaves and fish that satisfy all (John 4, 5). We will miss the hope and joy in the gift of having been called to follow Jesus, knowing he is more than enough for now and all eternity.

Just before Jesus called his disciples to self-denial, cross carrying, and following him, in Mark's gospel he had been deconstructing and reconstructing their image of "Messiah." Peter had been so horrified at the idea of

40. McIntyre, *Shape of Pneumatology*, 273.

41. MacDonald, "Imagination," 11.

42. Dearborn, *Baptized Imagination,* 92–93. See also Brooks's studies of those for whom images come before ideas, including Einstein, who "addressed problems by playing with imaginative, visual and physical sensations." Brooks, *Social Animal,* 168.

Jesus, the Messiah, giving into suffering and death that he rebuked the one he had just named "Messiah." One of the harshest rebukes in the Gospels is uttered by Jesus in response, "Get behind me Satan." He proceeds to identify the heart of Peter's problem, "You are setting your mind not on divine things but on human things" (Mark 8:33).

The Holy Spirit is with us to draw our minds and hearts to God's truth and ways through the cleansing and infilling of our imaginations. Hatred and dehumanization, according to Tutu, result from "an acute failure of vision."[43] We cannot cure that on our own. "Jesus is our hope for complete wholeness, for healing that is salvation. And that hope has already been accomplished. So we are constantly called to experience the truth about us: that we are the beloved of God."[44] That all people are the beloved of God.

The good news is that the Holy Spirit is with us to cleanse and heal our imaginations, to give us visions of ourselves as being held in God's loving gaze, even as a "mother looks lovingly at her newborn baby," writes Tutu. "In this way you can imagine, then experience, the loving gaze that God turns to us. As we allow ourselves to accept God's acceptance, we can begin to accept our own goodness and beauty. With each glimpse of our own beauty we can begin to see the goodness and beauty in others."[45] God would inspire us with the vision that, "God's love overshadows us all."[46] And God's presence is with us to cleanse, recreate, and catalyze us to live in light of this new creation reality.

One of the challenges for those of us who are comfortable with the power and prestige of the way things are, is that it takes a powerful catalyst to move us with Paul from the elitism of a certain view of chosenness to the acknowledgment that we are "foremost of sinners," while also deeply loved by God along with all of God's children. Brueggemann describes our "*totalizing ideology of exceptionalism* that precludes critique of our entitlements and self-regard. . . . In the contemporary Western world, that totalizing ideology takes the form of 'chosenness' of white Western superiority that guarantees privilege and precludes serious change."[47] He goes on to narrate the biblical pattern of change that occurs through both the act of relinquishment and the act of reception of the new world. For Paul this was a

43. Tutu, *Made for Goodness*, 196.

44. Ibid., 198.

45. Ibid.

46. Ibid., 198, 199.

47. Brueggemann, *Practice of Prophetic Imagination*, 131.

dramatic process of transformation. For most of us it requires a lifetime of prayerful openness to the Spirit, of facing the shadows that have warped and continue to warp our imaginations, and of gradual transformation into the likeness of Jesus Christ.

6

Facing the Shadows

As perchance carvers do not faces make,
But that away, which hid them there, do take,
Let Crosses so take what hid Christ in thee,
And be his Image, or not his, but He.[1]

Our hope lies . . . in the wisdom wherein we live and move and have our being.
Thence we hope for endless forms of beauty informed of truth. If the dark
portion of our own being were the origin of our imaginations, we might well
fear the apparition of such monsters as would be generated in the sickness of a
decay which could never feel—only declare—a slow return towards primeval
chaos. But the Maker is our Light.[2]

Though the Spirit imparts transformative visions to us, it is vital to
acknowledge that the imagination is also a reservoir of gruesome
and hideous images. The imagination, which can be a fountain of
beatific visions, can also be a seabed of monsters spawned by fear, pride,
hatred, despair, and even the demonic. What is it that arises within a person and thwarts the Spirit's new creation in faith, hope, and love? What

1. Donne, "From 'The Crosse.'"
2. MacDonald, "Imagination," 25. Cf. 2 Cor 4:6.

shadows arise in believers' perceptions to obscure their vision of God's re-creation of others? Reconciliation is often thwarted because of the natural tendency to perceive the "other" via distorting images, rather than by the power of the Spirit as a new creation. It is obvious that the imagination is no neutral or purely benign realm. The world of the imagination, connected with intuition and the unconscious, has a dark side also.

This is evident in Peter's own life. A significant journey is required before he is open and willing to see Cornelius no longer as defiling, but as a brother in Christ. He has to face numerous startling revelations about his own identity before he is able to receive his Acts 10 transforming and catalyzing vision, as described in chapter three. As previously noted, Peter initially had a rather idealized sense of himself, blurting out his ideas, strategies, and claims of unwavering loyalty with utter confidence. As David Benner writes, "It is . . . highly unlikely that he could have known the depths of his fears or the magnitude of his pride. These levels of knowing of self awaited deeper knowing of God."[3]

Jesus lovingly walks with Peter as humiliating revelations of his weaknesses arise like unbeckoned shadows from within him. These shadows confront Peter with his limitations and brokenness, and confirm his desperate need for Jesus. Jesus comes in truth and grace each time to help Peter experience the cleansing power of his unconditional love and an invitation to live with both a realistic sense of his frailty and hope in God's immense empowering love. The awareness of these inner shadows accompanied by Jesus' illuminating love prepare Peter to see others differently, no less worthy, broken, or human than himself.

Peter's pilgrimage reveals the challenging process of learning to walk in the humbling reality of one's needs and limitations and the empowering truth of God's love. Like walking, it is as if Peter must take a step forward in facing the shadows of fear and pride within him and another step forward in receiving God's radiant love that dispels the shadows and frees him to be more authentically himself. The humbling sense of his creaturely dependence on Jesus is something Peter has to learn again and again. He learns to face this dependence because it is bathed in the light of Jesus' acceptance and empowering love, and the transformed vision of what it means to be

---

3. Benner, *Gift of Being Yourself*, 27. In an illuminating way, Benner explores the interdependent ways in which Peter gradually grows both in knowledge of himself and of Jesus (ch. 1).

human. Jesus' life reveals that full humanity means utter dependence on God. "I do nothing but what I see the Father doing" (John 5:19).

Problems arise when we refuse to embrace God's loving exposure of our shadows of need and our creaturely dependence on God. Zacchaeus acknowledged and was liberated by such truth; Judas and the rich young ruler rejected it. Without acceptance of dependence on God's love, one can easily become vulnerable to the shadows that arise from the chasms of fear, pain, and alienation, and that promote delusions of grandeur and autonomy, which fracture relationships. We may even think we have embraced the love of God, but unless we also acknowledge and face the shadows from these chasms, we may in fact be living in unconscious reaction to them. An insidious twist occurs when, rather than letting God's love be the illuminating center of our lives, we try to exploit God's love for self-aggrandizement, which actually fuels rather than exposes shadows of fear and pride.

Unacknowledged shadows have tremendous power in our lives. And as Brooks writes, "People overestimate their ability to control their unconscious tendencies."[4] The mistake has been to think that it is possible to reason or will one's way out of these lurking shadows. "The conscious mind simply lacks the strength and awareness to directly control unconscious processes."[5] Brooks writes that on occasion, reason and will are able to "resist temptation and control the impulses. But in many cases they are simply too weak to impose self-discipline by themselves. In many cases self-delusion takes control."[6]

One need not look far to see examples of unacknowledged shadows and self-delusion in the church. Among numerous outspoken leaders who can offer many reasons and motivations for avoiding certain immoral behaviors, there are noteworthy examples of some of these same leaders falling into the very traps against which they have so vigorously applied the forces of reason and will. It takes little effort to think of Christian leaders who rail against greed, pornography, or infidelity, only to be caught in that behavior at some point. Rohr warns, "Invariably when something upsets you, and you have a strong emotional reaction out of proportion to the moment, your shadow self has just been exposed."[7]

4. Brooks, *Social Animal*, 219.

5. Ibid., 125.

6. Ibid., 127.

7. Rohr, *Falling Upward*, 133.

Peter was upset by the suggestion that he might betray Jesus, and adamantly claimed he would die with Jesus before he would do such a thing (Matt 26:35). Peter had not fully faced the shadow of fear within him that was able to thwart his courageous intentions and his sense of Jesus' love in Peter's moment of trial. As mentioned previously, for Peter the gift of walking with Jesus was the invitation to face and acknowledge those shadows in himself, so that he could learn to lean humbly on God's power within him rather than relying on his own presumed strength. Ultimately Peter is only freed from the power of these shadows through extreme failure, the experience of Jesus' forgiving love, the infilling power of the Holy Spirit, and a transformed imagination.

Dominant Western culture, with its emphasis on rationalism, has not promoted great attentiveness to the shadow side of life. Rationalism has been seen as a force of illumination to keep the shadows at bay and under control. Granted, rationalism has been the source of much scientific discovery and technological advance. But as Brooks writes, "It is blind to the influence of unconscious. . . . Rationalism looks at the conscious mind, and assumes that that is all there is. It cannot acknowledge the importance of unconscious processes, because once it dips its foot in that dark and bottomless current, all hope of regularity and predictability is gone."[8]

Narratives That Clarify and Cleanse

The imagination can serve as a helpful vehicle to unlock the unconscious realm and to bring clarity to the issues that shadows pose. I want to explore two narratives by MacDonald that are particularly illuminating about the challenges of facing the shadows and moving toward reconciliation. One is a short story and the other is *Phantastes*, mentioned earlier in this book.

"Photogen and Nycteris"

MacDonald's short story, "The History of Photogen and Nycteris," exposes some of the rationalist predilections and pitfalls of dominant Western culture.[9] It illustrates the ways in which narratives from the baptized imagination can reach and expose the shadows in each of us. This story

8. Brooks, *Social Animal*, 226, 227.
9. MacDonald, *The Golden Key and Other Stories*, 36–86.

also highlights the damaging impact unacknowledged shadows can have on relationships to foster isolation and alienation.

In the story, two children, a white boy and a dark-skinned girl, are taken as babies and raised in extreme conditions by a witch scientist, Watho, who experiments on them to gain more knowledge. Watho "cared for nothing in itself—only for knowing it."[10] The boy, Photogen, is exposed exclusively to the light and the girl, Nycteris, to the darkness. Photogen's training helps him to grow in confidence that he can master anything and that there is no enemy he cannot vanquish. He is given the privileges of access, education, and power, and as long as it is daylight, he is free to explore as far and wide as he desires. His mentor, Fargu, is charged with training him and ensuring that he is home before sundown, and never has to see his shadow. Photogen reflects Rohr's depiction of Western males: "Men are actually encouraged to deny their shadow self in any competitive society . . ."[11]

On the other hand, Nycteris's entire existence is lived in the shadows. Though she is given little education, still she teaches herself to read, and grows in yearning to move beyond the narrow confines of the dark crypt in which she has been confined. She yearns for more light than that which shines from her alabaster lamp. She has to challenge and push beyond the constricting structures of her life in order to develop as a person.

MacDonald's story portrays powerfully the restricted existence women and people of color experienced in nineteenth-century England. Nineteenth-century political, social, and scientific theorists concluded that, like people with darker skin, "Women, the lower classes, and criminals were also childlike, or savage in certain ways. All were subordinates in different realms of life, all lacked the ability to look after or control themselves, and all represented lower positions on the unilinear scale."[12] It was considered dangerous to educate "Negroes and women."[13] Scientific studies were done to document the inferior intellectual capacities of these groups, and to confirm the superior intellectual abilities of Anglo-Saxon males.[14] Herbert Spencer "maintained that the higher the race, the greater the con-

10. Ibid., 36.

11. Rohr, *Falling Upward*, 135.

12. Jackson and Weidman, "Race and Evolution," 83.

13. Ibid., 83.

14. Ibid., 61–96. MacDonald so objected to these views that he tutored women and taught at a women's college. Dearborn, *Baptized Imagination*, 21.

trast between men and women in physical appearance and social role."[15] Ultimately because they were often kept in the shadows, women and people of color were typically associated with that which is shadowy, mysterious, and frightening.

MacDonald's story also portrays the crippling impact of being raised with the delusion of control and blindness to the shadows and unconscious depths both within and beyond us. Photogen is like a man living in a house for much of his life, unaware of the trap door that opens up to level after level beneath him.[16] When Photogen strays beyond his allotted boundaries of daylight and encounters night for the first time, he falls through that trap door and is devastated. Emotions surface which he has never had to face—fear, lack of control, isolation, inadequacy, shame, humiliation, and impotence.

His identity is shaken to the core and he has to face the false self with which he has come to identify. He had been the center of his world and life, and in the liminal experience of this unforeseen mystery he realizes how feeble and dependent he is. He even has to lean on the courage, compassion, and strength of the dark female, Nycteris, who has made her way out of her tomb and is glorying in the light of the moon and the caress of the wind. She is not afraid of shadows, powerlessness, or mystery—for she has grown up in humble circumstances without the illusion of control. Her identity has developed in ways that acknowledge limits and shadows, and her yearning is for greater illumination and connection to the world around her. Thus, she is able to extend mercy and help in Photogen's great time of need.

Whereas Nycteris sees commonality with this fellow creature and mistakes him for a fellow girl (having never before seen a male), Photogen is deeply offended. He seeks to distinguish himself as superior to all others, and especially to this girl. He is even more offended when she says, "Oh I see! . . . No of course! You can't be a girl: girls are not afraid without reason. I understand now: it is because you are not a girl that you are so frightened."[17] He twists and writhes at this comment and then blames "this horrible darkness . . . [that] makes me behave like a girl."[18] He has a fixed

15. Jackson and Weidman, "Race and Evolution," 82.

16. Brooks, *Social Animal*, 204.

17. MacDonald, *The Golden Key and Other Stories*, 66.

18. Ibid.

category for girls and it is the category of weakness and fearfulness, and a fixed category for himself, strong and invincible.

Photogen is repelled by anything beyond his mastery that exposes his limits, his dependency, and his shame. Rather than face these realities, he seeks to flee them and return to the delusion of his own grandeur. Because he hates these shadows in himself, he lacks empathy for Nycteris when she is overwhelmed with terror in her first exposure to the sun. When the sun rises, after she has cared for him throughout his terrifying night, he abandons her and glories in the return of his own confidence and prowess.

In this story MacDonald reveals that relationships of mutual interdependence and respect are thwarted by a refusal of one's own limitations and vulnerabilities. Similarly Bonhoeffer writes, "The grace of the other person's being our helper who is a partner because he or she helps us to bear our limit . . . this grace becomes a curse" when approached with pride and rebellion.[19] Nycteris is there to bear Photogen's limit with him, but because he rejects his limits and shadows, he also rejects her and any shared nature with her. He uses her for the time of his great need, but rebukes her when she faces her own fear of the sun: "'What is the matter with you, girl?' said Photogen, with the arrogance of all male creatures until they have been taught by the other kind."[20]

Photogen's freedom only comes when he is humble enough to see himself more honestly and to see Nycteris with all the gifts and strengths she has to offer. After much suffering and through the love of Nycteris, he is able to face the shadows of pride, shame, and weakness in himself and to recognize his common humanity with one he has seen as "other." Through their ultimate reconciliation, both are enabled to love what they had previously feared and empowered together to overcome the true evil attempting to destroy their lives.

MacDonald demonstrates in this story that shadows are not necessarily evil, but can serve as helpful indicators of our interior life and our need for God and for others. Shadows can serve to remind you that you are not the light, but rather in need of God's loving radiance and power, and that you share common limitations with all people. The challenge is, first, to be able to acknowledge the shadows and see through them to the fuller reality

19. Bonhoeffer, *Creation and Fall*, 99.

20. MacDonald, *The Golden Key and Other Stories*, 69. Nycteris resonates with Brooks's protagonist, Erica, who is raised up by God to "jostle the White Man from the comfort of his categories and help him see hidden forces that actually drive the mind." Brooks, *Social Animal*, 170.

of our interdependency, and second, to refuse to allow shadows to cut us off from God and others in shame, pride, and denial. Ultimately MacDonald reveals that true freedom is living in responsiveness to the light and in interconnectedness with those who may seem other, yet with whom one is bound at the deepest levels of existence.

MacDonald's story also challenges the exaltation of reason as of supreme value. Reason, when used to gain power over others, is revealed as a force of division, compartmentalization, and disintegration. Reason, disconnected from imagination and love, becomes an unfettered wolf in Watho's mind and ultimately transforms her entire being into a wolf that seeks to devour everyone around her for self-aggrandizement.[21] Thus MacDonald reveals the limitations of rationalism through both the devastation caused by Watho and through Photogen's inability to deal with the inexplicable and emotional aspects of life.

Unfortunately mainstream Western Christianity, with fears about excessive introspection and "psychobabble," and a desire to be credible in the larger rationalistic context, has not empowered people to do much shadow work. Rather, many Christians have joined in efforts to exalt reason and will and to evade self-reflection, thus perpetuating the promotion of false selves or hypocrisy. As Benner writes, "While concepts such as self-discovery, identity and authenticity are easily dismissed as mere psychobabble, each has an important role to play in the transformational journey of Christian spirituality."[22]

The baptized imagination fueled by the Holy Spirit can bear truth into the depths of our beings to reveal the shadows of shame, fear, pride, and self-delusion. As Lewis wrote, the imagination is a way of "smuggling truth."[23] It can bring light and healing from the addictions, destructive behaviors, and the fracturing of lives and communities that unacknowledged shadows provoke. It can silence the voice of shame that feeds off of secrecy and criticalness and produces alienation.[24]

---

21. MacDonald lived during the early debates around Darwinian evolution. As a person who loved science and believed that all truth is God's truth, his faith was not threatened by theories of evolution. Rather he was far more concerned about the ways in which scientific materialism and hyper-rationalism promoted the devolution of human character and society.

22. Benner, *Gift of Being Yourself*, 13.

23. Lewis, "Letter to Sister Penelope," 262.

24. Brown, *Daring Greatly*, 77–78.

Phantastes

MacDonald explores the issues of shadows even more fully in *Phantastes*, mentioned in the introduction of this book, to which Lewis attributed the baptism of his own imagination.[25] Anodos in *Phantastes* provides an example of a person who is oblivious to the dangers and destructiveness of his attendant shadow. He experiences the grace of God repeatedly, yet he continually violates this grace and fails to honor and learn from God's gracious messengers. He is nurtured, loved, bathed, and renewed time after time. Costly love is shown to him, whether through the beech-tree's sacrifice of her "hair" or the old woman of the cottage's sacrifice of herself. Despite having to face his failures again and again, despite repeated baptisms of mercy, he remains relatively unchanged.

MacDonald's descriptions of Anodos's shadow are very instructive. Anodos's shadow initially emerges in his life when he narcissistically refuses to heed the warnings of others, and is unwilling to acknowledge or live within his limits.[26] It's an ancient story. The shadow that emerges has its most painful impact on his relationships, creating distortions, suspicion, and the denigration of others. It keeps him isolated and alienated from others and tethered to the delusion of self-sufficiency, which in turn provides fertile ground for the shadow's expanding power over him. MacDonald depicts numerous ways in which an unaddressed shadow destructively impacts lives and relationships.

The Ways of the Shadow

LOSS OF WONDER

The first impact for Anodos is a loss of the wonder that was awakening in him in the new realm to which he had been led. Just as he is about to reach out to a lovely child in awe and respect, the shadow rises up in him to darken his perception. Anodos explains, "Once as I passed by a cottage,

25. "Remember, the opposite of the rational is not always irrational, but it can also be *transrational* or bigger than the rational mind can process; . . . The transrational has the capacity to keep us inside an open system and a larger horizon so that the soul, the heart, and the mind do not close down inside of small and constricted space." Rohr, *Falling Upward*, xxxi.

26. This is particularly relevant with the "epidemic of narcissism" that abounds in our society according to Brown. Brown, *Daring Greatly*, 20–22.

there came out a lovely fairy child, with two wondrous toys, one in each hand. . . . Round the child's head was an aureole of emanating rays. As I looked at him in wonder and delight, round crept from behind me the something dark, and the child stood in my shadow. Straightway he was a commonplace boy. . . . I sighed and departed."[27] The shadow within him thwarts Anodos's ability to see the other with awe and delight.

ISOLATION AND ALIENATION

Second, it inhibits his freedom to be known by others. Anodos allows the shadow to keep him from trusting even a humble, caring knight who had helped him previously. In this way, the healing that could come from confessing his failures to the knight and being known is thwarted.[28] Anodos had been traveling with the knight for two days and was beginning to love him. "Shame at my neglect of his warning, and a horror which shrunk from even alluding to its cause, kept me silent, till, on the evening of the second day, some noble words from my companion roused all my heart; and I was at the point of falling on his neck, and telling him the whole story, seeking if not for helpful advice, for of that I was hopeless, yet for the comfort of sympathy—when round slid the shadow and inwrapt my friend; and I could not trust him. The glory of his brow vanished; the light of his eye grew cold; and I held my peace. The next morning we parted."[29]

ARROGANCE AND PRIDE

Third, Anodos's unchecked shadow fuels a sense of superiority in him. Rather than provoking concern about its negative impact, the shadow causes him to take pride in his "realism" and the shadow's ability to disenchant the world.[30] "But the most dreadful thing of all was, that I now began to feel something like satisfaction in the presence of my shadow. I began to be rather vain of my attendant, saying to myself, 'In a land like this, with so many illusions everywhere, I need his aid to disenchant the things around

27. MacDonald, *Phantastes*, 60.

28. Ibid.

29. Ibid., 60–61. MacDonald's depiction correlates powerfully with Brown's research, which traces the unwillingness to be vulnerable to shame and the silence off which it feeds. See, for example, Brown, *Daring Greatly*, 63–65.

30. MacDonald, *Phantastes*, 61.

me. He does away with all appearances, and shows me things in their true colour and form. And I am not one to be fooled with the vanities of the common crowd. I will not see beauty where there is none. I will dare to behold things as they are. And if I live in a waste instead of a paradise, I will love knowing where I live."[31]

MacDonald reveals the ways in which the shadow destroys Anodos's ability to see others, himself, and the world sacramentally. No longer does he have the bi-focal vision of grace from the Spirit to see beyond appearances to the glory in and behind all things. No longer is he free to delight in others or in the world of God's creation. As Rohr writes, "The shadow self invariably presents itself as something like prudence, common sense, justice, or 'I am doing this for your good,' when it is actually manifesting fear, control, manipulation, or even vengeance."[32]

Thus, Saul failed to see Stephen's "face like an angel" or to believe his wondrous words of Israel's history and fulfillment in Jesus, and instead stood by approvingly as he was stoned to death (Acts 6:15 –8:1). Even so, police set dogs and fire hoses on protesters and failed to challenge lynchings in the civil rights era of the US, responses paralleled by governments' treatment of dissenters around the world. The shadows of fear, pride, and power rise and obscure the ability to see the other as a miracle of God's creation to be honored and protected. As Benner writes, "Sensing its fundamental unreality, the false self wraps itself in experience—experiences of power, pleasure and honor. Intuiting that it is but a shadow, it seeks to convince itself of its reality by equating itself with what it does and achieves."[33]

Benner describes the way in which the hollowness created by the shadow's relational casualties fosters ravenous hunger. "Because it is hollow at the core, the life of a false self is a life of excessive attachments."[34] Thus relationships are not only compromised and wounded by the shadow's ability to obscure the sacramental humanity of the other, the emptiness such alienation produces also makes one want to exploit, possess, and consume what the other has.

---

31. One hears echoes of this attitude in C. S. Lewis's dwarves in *The Last Battle* who refuse to "be taken in" and thus cannot see the kingdom of God in their midst. Lewis, *The Last Battle*, ch. 13.

32. Rohr, *Falling Upward*, 133.

33. Benner, *Gift of Being Yourself*, 81.

34. Ibid.

Unacknowledged and unchecked shadows create alienation and isolation, which then foster ravenous hunger and greed as ways to fill the emptiness or numb the pain. Brené Brown calls this a hunger for "shadow comforts."[35] MacDonald portrays such a progression in the impact of the shadow on Anodos. He encounters a "little maiden . . . almost a woman" who is singing and dancing and carrying her greatest treasure, a musical globe.[36] They meet at bright noon and walk together each day until twilight for three days. Anodos grows increasingly enchanted with her and her globe. The third day as they walk on till evening, "The shadow glided round and inwrapt the maiden. It could not change her. But my desire to know about the globe, which in his gloom began to waver as with an inward light, and to shoot out flashes of many-coloured flame, grew irresistible."[37]

Anodos seizes the globe and despite her tears, protest, and prayers he will not release it. He fights her for it until it eventually explodes in his hands and "a black vapour broke upwards from out of it; then turned, as if blown sideways, and enveloped the maiden, hiding even the shadow in its blackness."[38] The violated maiden flees with the fragments, wailing, "You have broken my globe; my globe is broken, ah my globe."[39] Anodos's greed for this shadow comfort has fostered disintegration of his character and destruction of the other. As Benner writes, "Attachments imprison us in falsity as we follow the flickering sirens of desire."[40]

Anodos has violated her and destroyed her greatest treasure, not because he is a malicious person, but because he is a person who has failed to live within his limits, to humbly listen to the wisdom of others, and to deal with his shadow. Similarly Bonhoeffer writes, Adam and Eve's refusal to live within the grace of their limits resulted in "shame and obsessive desire."[41] They felt the urge to flee, to hide, and to live in violation of rather than protection of the other. What began as wonder, mutuality, and interdependence became competition, blaming, and grasping.

---

35. Brown, *Daring Greatly*, 147.

36. MacDonald, *Phantastes*, 61.

37. Ibid., 62.

38. Ibid.

39. Ibid.

40. Benner, *Gift of Being Yourself*, 82.

41. Bonhoeffer, *Creation and Fall*, 133.

So powerful does the influence of the shadow become in Anodos's life that whenever he even draws close to another person, "the whole appearance of the person began to change; and this change increased in degree as I approached."[42] He describes the nature of the change as "grotesque," in which the other becomes "absurdly hideous."[43] He loses interest in other people "for the shadow was in my heart as well as at my heels."[44]

As Richard Rohr writes, it is critical to face your shadow, because your shadow self "is like a double-blindness, keeping you from seeing—and being—your best and deepest self."[45] What does such double-blindness look like and how can it be faced and overcome? Jesus described it graphically as having a log in one's eye. It includes first an unwillingness to be honest about oneself and thus to be caught in self-delusion and denial. "I'm not racist" is a fairly common example of such self-delusion.

Double-blindness also includes the distorted ways in which we see others. Jesus said, "You hypocrite, first take the log out of your own eye, and then you will see clearly to take the speck out of your neighbor's eye" (Matt 7:5). Aspects of cultural conditioning can trigger shadows of fear, pride, and refusal of the other. David Brooks describes the way in which triggers of disgust and fear are evident across cultures. "Finally, and most problematically, there is the in-group/loyalty concern. Humans segregate themselves into groups. They feel visceral loyalty to members of their group, no matter how arbitrary the basis for membership, and feel visceral disgust toward those who violate loyalty codes."[46]

The Restorative Process of Grace

THE GRACE OF RENEWED VISION

What revives Anodos from gloom, blindness, and alienation is grace in the form of a small stream flowing from the desert, which he follows until it becomes a broad river and takes him to an idealized palace of grace and renewal. Though his shadow does not initially enter there, he is given a vision of the impact of shadows on relationships through the literature he

---

42. MacDonald, *Phantastes*, 63.

43. Ibid.

44. Ibid., 64.

45. Rohr, *Falling Upward*, 128.

46. Brooks, *Social Animal*, 287.

literally enters into in the library. This temporary escape from the daily challenges of his pilgrimage gives him hope of what could be, but is not enough to transform him. It gives him a respite, but the shadow in his heart still motivates him to overstep his limits. Though he is able to sing his beloved into visibility, he is so enthralled by the one he reveals that he defies the law of the place, "Do not touch," and grasps her into his arms. She feels violated and flees from him as well. Clearly, renewed vision is a gracious gift but not enough to transform. To see what is possible is not necessarily empowerment for living its promise.

MacDonald poignantly describes the shame, depression, and self-loathing that follows as a "torturous descent" into an underground realm where Anodos says, "Darker grew my thoughts till at last I had no hope."[47] He has entered a grim underworld abyss of "sepulchral illumination,"[48] evil taunts, and hideous mockery. Goblins swarm around him, derisively attacking him with a "galvanic torrent" of a "battery of malevolence."[49] He trudges on and on through a "country of rock" that narrows more and more tightly around him, and a gray mist that swallows up the way behind him. MacDonald's description of the impact of failure and shame correlates powerfully with twelve years of research on shame by sociologist Brené Brown. Rather than fostering courage and connection with others, "Shame sends the gremlins to fill our heads with completely different messages of: . . . You're not good enough!"[50]

GRACE OF BAPTISM

Ultimately Anodos's way leads out of the cavern to the shores of a wintry sea and a "dismal day, more dismal even than the day I had left."[51] Anodos, in an act of utter self-abandonment, plunges into the sea, which rather than consuming his life is a baptism into grace: "a blessing, like the kiss of a mother" alighting on his "soul, a calm, deeper than that which accompanies a hope deferred, bathed my spirit."[52]

47. MacDonald, *Phantastes*, 119.
48. Ibid., 123.
49. Ibid., 120.
50. Brown, *Daring Greatly*, 66.
51. MacDonald, *Phantastes*, 125.
52. Ibid., 126.

The sea carries him to the old woman of the cottage who welcomes him in, nurses him like a sick child, and feeds him "like a baby."[53] She gives him access to doorways of revelation into his past and present life. He is able to face his past pain and failure, and present lack of fulfillment, in this context of love and acceptance. Then, she tries to warn him and prevent him from entering into the "door of the Timeless."[54] But he refuses to honor this beloved woman with her brown parchment-like skin and radiant eyes. Instead he rejects her warning, pushes past her, and plunges through the "door of the Timeless" to pursue his own interest. Her rescue of him from this place of no return costs her freedom and immense suffering, including a year of burial under water in her cottage. He is desolate and full of remorse, but still so untransformed. It is evident that just as renewed vision is insufficient, even so self-abandonment and self-awareness are not enough to empower transformation in Anodos's life.

THE SPIRIT AND THE SHADOW

MacDonald's story points to a deeper reason why it is only through the power of the Holy Spirit cleansing and liberating the imagination that deep transformation takes place. It is not enough merely to acknowledge the ways in which shadows continue to blur our vision and blind us to the truth of our selfish destructiveness. It is not enough to experience the baptism of relinquishment, and receive more clarity about our lives. Anodos needs supernatural power to face and challenge the shadows that obscure the vision of his interconnectedness with all of life, and which urge self-delusion and self-aggrandizement instead. He needs a new dynamism to stop approaching others through the framework of Buber's "I-it," in order to see them in an "I-thou" way.

So what does it take to address the shadows that continually rise up within to subvert our best efforts and closest relationships, let alone relationships that are deeply fractured and in need of healing? What happens when the shadows continue to grow in power because of prideful efforts to ignore them or self-centered desires to indulge them?

As Rohr conveys, the goal of faith is liberation from "the closing prison-house of the false self. Many have said before me that spirituality is much more about unlearning than learning, because the 'growing boy' is

53. Ibid., 129.

54. Ibid., 144.

usually growing into major illusions, all of which must be undone to free him from prison and take him back to his beginnings in God. 'Unless you change, and become like a little child, you will not enter the kingdom of God,' Jesus says (Matt 18:3)."[55] What is it that brings such a powerful and liberating release from the shadows, beyond renewed vision, relinquishment, and greater honesty, to produce childlike trust and humility?

MacDonald reflects a fairly lengthy process in Anodos, who moves from one event to the other, working hard to be ever more faithful and valiant. Sadly his successes tend to feed his shadow self of pride and vanity. Ultimately his shadow becomes such a powerful idealized self (the knight he strove to be), that Anodos is powerless to resist it. Anodos hears a voice of warning within to resist or become its slave, but having oriented himself to listen to it for so long he gives in. He allows it to lead him to a dreary windowless tower where he is shut in by and with his horrible shadow.

Anodos's story reveals that if we refuse to face these shadows, or the false self, we begin to equate ourselves with the shadows. Eventually one can devolve into the persona fabricated from the shadows. Lewis describes this process in *The Great Divorce,* in the encounter of the glorious Susan Smith with her husband, who is a shrunken figure chained to a tragedian. The tragedian dramatically dominates the conversation in ways that are dripping with self-pity and reflect the projected persona of her husband, until the false self eventually completely absorbs the ever-shrinking reality of what had once been her husband.

Rohr writes, "If you have spent many years building your particular tower of success and self-importance—your personal 'salvation project,' as Thomas Merton called it—or have successfully constructed your own superior ethnic group, religion, or 'house,' you won't want to leave it."[56]

For Anodos the only light in his self-made prison comes from a small opening above. He is now living the autonomous reality he allowed his shadow to shape: "Now I was indeed in pitiful plight. There was literally nothing in the tower but my shadow and me."[57] Even so, grace is able to reach him there. Though during the day he is miserable, at night the light of the moon (for MacDonald, a symbol of Christ) transforms his prison into a place of natural beauty and relational richness.[58] The moon's light offers

---

55. Rohr, *Falling Upward,* 99–100.

56. Ibid., 21.

57. MacDonald, *Phantastes,* 161.

58. See Dearborn, *Baptized Imagination,* 69, 80.

visions of those who have loved him and reminds him of the loveliness of his encounters with them and with creation. The light awakens love within him and a yearning for greater childlikeness and true freedom.

What ultimately frees Anodos is the light of Christ and the forgiving and empowering presence of the Holy Spirit via the girl whose magic globe he had destroyed. After being prepared by the light of the moon, release from captivity comes to Anodos via a song of forgiveness, which MacDonald conveys in ways that evoke the healing presence of the Holy Spirit. "Like a living soul, like an incarnation of Nature, the song entered my prison-house. Each tone folded its wings, and laid itself, like a caressing bird, upon my heart. It bathed me like a sea; inwrapt me like an odorous vapour; entered my soul like a long draught of clear spring-water; shone upon me like essential sunlight; soothed me like a mother's voice and hand."[59] His description of this fuller baptism of the Spirit offers a corollary kind of antidote to the shadow's destructive ways of enwrapping others to defile and distort their being. This is a cleansing and healing experience, even as the odorous vapor of love surrounds him (in contrast to the vapor that arose when he broke the young girl's globe), and he is able to experience the wonder of "essential sunlight."[60] The song is a tribute to the sun and to the nourishment of Mother earth and ends with an invitation to Anodos to join in the celebration: "From the narrow desert, O man of pride, Come into the house, so high and wide."[61]

Anodos is enthralled by the music and is empowered simply to open the door. "Why had I not done so before? I did not know."[62] The singer reveals that she is the very girl whom he had violated when he grasped and broke her precious globe. "Did you not know me? But you hurt me, and that I suppose, makes it easy for a man to forget."[63] Though she never recovered what was lost, she had taken the broken pieces to the Fairy Queen who had laid them aside, and urged her to sleep in a great white hall with black pillars and red curtains. She has awakened to a new reality—no enchanting globe of music, but rather the ability to sing with a heart bursting with joy in ways that "do good, and deliver people. And now I have delivered

59. MacDonald, *Phantastes*, 162–63.

60. The sun for MacDonald offered an analogy of the Father, as the moon stood for Jesus Christ. See Dearborn, *Baptized Imagination*, 69, 80.

61. MacDonald, *Phantastes*, 164

62. Ibid.

63. Ibid.

you, and I am so happy."[64] Anodos is humbled, but also freed from a "great weight." He kneels before her and begs for forgiveness, but she has already forgiven him. Her life is now spent traveling through the dim forest bringing deliverance to others imprisoned in the darkness.

Anodos is freed not only from guilt and shame, but also from his false self. Rather than looking down on her as an object to be exploited, she is now a source of inspiration and aspiration for him. "Between her and me there was a great gulf. She was uplifted, by sorrow and well-doing, into a region I could hardly hope ever to enter. I watched her departure, as one watches a sunset. She went like a radiance through the dark wood, which was henceforth bright to me, from simply knowing that such a creature was in it. She was bearing the sun to the unsunned spots. The light and the music of her broken globe were now in her heart and her brains."[65]

In a way, Anodos died and was reborn through the Holy Spirit's enfolding him in forgiving love. His shadow self lost its grip on him and he became a liberated and transformed person at last. He relinquished the illusion of himself as a great knight and shed his armor of invulnerability. He embraces his true identity at last. "Then first I knew the delight of being lowly, of saying to myself, 'I am what I am, nothing more.' 'I have failed,' I said, 'I have lost myself—would it have been my shadow.' I looked round: the shadow was nowhere to be seen. Ere long, I learned that it was not myself, but only my shadow, that I had lost. I learned that it is better, a thousand-fold, for a proud man to fall and be humbled, than to hold up his head in his pride and fancied innocence. . . . Another self seemed to arise, like a white spirit from a dead man, from the dumb and trampled self of the past. Doubtless this self must again die and be buried, and again, from its tomb, spring a winged child."[66] Thus Anodos is free at last to be a humble squire to one who had been his rival, to discern truth from falsehood and ultimately to give his life in service of the truth, knowing he must die to himself again and again.

Ultimately it is God's presence and power through forgiving love that both exposes the shadows and sets us free—free from hubris for humility, free from autonomy for love, and free from noble illusions for authentic freedom and service.

64. Ibid.
65. Ibid., 165.
66. Ibid., 166.

The story of Anodos reveals that it is no facile process to move out of a false identity that is both imprisoning for others and for oneself. Baptism into Christ is part of the process for Christians, but for new creation to fully emerge we are summoned to continually welcome the Holy Spirit's transformation of the imagination, and to receive the Spirit's empowerment through repeated death to new ways of life. As Nouwen writes, our lives are "a long process of mortification."[67]

Owning one's sins and shadows and being willing to receive the double-edged sword of forgiveness is crucial for those who are perpetrators. For those who are the survivors and victims, the call is to step out of the shadows more fully into the light—to let the light define rather than the shadows. The former moves from false dignity through death and forgiveness to new creation; the latter from false death to dignity of the new creation, and the power to offer forgiveness that liberates the oppressor.

Through the gift of the imagination, MacDonald has conveyed profound truths about the long ordeal necessary to cleanse the toxic well from which relationships are repeatedly poisoned and the costly process by which Christ's gift of reconciliation becomes lived reality among God's people. As in the biblical witness, the last shall be first and the least shall be the greatest of all. Those who think they are strong become imprisoned in their own self-aggrandizement, and it takes those who have been wounded by them to set them free. As the survivors carry the fragments of their shattered lives to the Healer, they are given a glorious voice to announce healing and forgiveness to the perpetrators.

John Perkins offers a profound example of this in recent history. Having experienced the horrors of racism, which included the brutal murder of his brother, and a vicious beating that landed him in the hospital, he had to decide whether to stew in the shadows of hatred and bitterness or to let Christ's illuminating love break him free from this prison. By the power of the Holy Spirit he was able to take the shattered pieces of his broken body and broken dignity and offer them to the Lord. God put a new song in his heart, a song of deliverance, and of taking light into dark places. Perkins offered forgiveness to the white pastors whose churches excluded him, and he continues to communicate grace and truth to Christians around the world. As one example, he created the Christian Community Development Association, which brings people together across race, ethnicity, gender, and class to share in God's kingdom work of healing, justice, and reconciliation.

67. Nouwen, *A Letter of Consolation*, 42.

This is the biblical pattern. It is the wounded one who becomes the healer. God was the offended party, yet becomes the fount of all grace and forgiveness in Christ. Jesus was denied three times by Peter, but bears liberation to him—turning him into a central leader of the early church. Shadows can have profound destructive power, but the recreating power of the Spirit brings release and freedom and can forge bonds of love and redemption even out of deepest pain.

7

Signposts and Oases of the New Creation

For the Lord your God is bringing you into a good land, a land with flowing
streams, with springs and underground waters welling up in valleys and hills.
(Deut 8:7)

Each one of us is now a part of his resurrection body, refreshed and
sustained at one fountain—his Spirit—where we all come to drink.
(1 Cor 12:13, *The Message*)

The central thesis of this book is that the Holy Spirit is God's abiding
presence to draw all people to the renewing waters of Christ's re-
creating and reconciling work and life. Because of the Spirit's universal, life-giving, and particularized presence, these waters are available
even in the most turbulent and seemingly desolate places. Furthermore,
I have proposed that the channels in which these waters often flow most
freely, at least initially, are those of the imagination. It is through the imagination that God's Spirit carries creativity, hope, and love into our hearts
when there may be rational and psychological objections that would otherwise obstruct them. As water can seep through rigid barriers and wear
down long-standing walls, even so the renewing grace of the Holy Spirit
finds a route via the imagination past the intellectual and psychological
constructs that can isolate us from God and others. The Spirit can bring

cleansing where the shadowy debris of relational wounds clings. And hope can burst forth that, even as God calls us the beloved, God would open up to us the rich wonder of life with beloved brothers and sisters from every tribe, tongue, and nation.

The life-giving dynamism of God's grace flows deeply underneath the relational deserts of our world, offering springs from which seeds of new creation are watered and oases where God's kingdom becomes visible. As mentioned previously, the imagination offers the gift of bi-focal sight making it possible to sustain visions of both the desert and the hidden wells of new life. The Holy Spirit uses our imaginations to bring us refreshing tastes of this real living water in the midst of scorching heat and the turmoil of our world. The polar tensions that the imagination sustains between divergent realities provide a rich and redemptive dynamic from which new life emerges.

These dynamic tensions include the presence of the kingdom undergirding all things, though ongoing pain and suffering still exists; the fact that God reigns and all authority on heaven and on earth has been granted to Christ, and yet so many other powers seems to dominate our political, economic, social, and personal landscape; the deep peace of knowing that all things have been reconciled in Christ, and yet the anguish of so many torn relationships and communities; confidence that all will be well, with active restlessness to participate by the Spirit in God penetrating the world with renewing grace until all is well. The rich bi-focal capacity of the imagination that can see beyond either/or to both-and perspectives offers a vessel through which God's people may receive God's redemptive and reconciling love, be catalyzed by dynamic hope, and share this love and hope with others in the most tumultuous and fragmented situations.

Furthermore, the Holy Spirit makes possible an imaginative leap from seeing only the broken and obvious places of the world to perceiving the kingdom of God flowing beneath all things. The Spirit draws us into prayer and encounters with oases that spring up from those who have entered into the life of Christ by the Spirit. As Rob Wall writes, "To wait for the Spirit, then, is to await the Spirit who empowers believers to continue 'all that Jesus had begun to do and teach' (Acts 1:1)."[1]

The new life that the Spirit redemptively creates signals to others the way to God's springs of living water. It would seem foolish when journeying through the desert to ignore signs directing you to the wells of life-giving

---

1. Wall, "Waiting on the Holy Spirit," 42.

water or to the oases that flourish from this water. Similarly it makes no sense if your desire is to travel homeward to speed through city after city, ignoring the signs that point you to your final destination. The Spirit has offered many image-rich signs of the kingdom in order to draw people to the wells of God's new creation and to sustain them on the journey homeward to fullness of life with God, God's people, and God's creation.

Often these signs have been forgotten or ignored, as Eustace and Jill ignored Aslan's signs for them in Lewis's *The Silver Chair*. Thus, like them the church has frequently detoured to the "Harfangs" of history, places of comfort and ease, but where giants lurk to devour. Yet even though we are drawn to shadow comforts, the signs still lead God's people to places of personal liberation and the gift of sharing in God's liberation of others from darkness and despair to experience the glories of God's "Narnia" reign over communities once again.

I would like to highlight three of these signposts of God's new creation and then describe four historical oases of Christian renewal that have flourished because God's people responded to the Spirit's invitation and honored these signs as from the Spirit. In these movements God's people not only drank deeply from the springs to which they pointed, but also sought others to join them as well. The three signposts are *ecclesia, koinonia,* and sacrament, and four oases I have chosen to highlight are the early church, Celtic Christianity, the Wesleyan revival, and the contemporary Pentecostal movement.

Signposts

In ways that express the dynamism of the Spirit's creativity, Christians were inspired to take cultural frameworks shaped by some of the most fragmenting forces of Greco-Roman society and re-create them as images of God's reconciling kingdom. The Spirit of God was able to transform the very structures of Rome to create signposts that point to renewed life rather than crushing oppression and death. Cultural paradigms that stood for exclusion and division were transformed into new wineskins for the joyful new wine of the kingdom. This is especially exemplified in the signposts of *ekklesia, koinonia* and *sacramentum.*

Ekklesia

In classical Greek *ekklesia* was a political term that meant an exclusive, regularly summoned legislative body or assembly of citizens to do the work of the empire.[2] "Authorization to participate and the methods of summoning the assembly and of voting . . . were strictly regulated."[3] Slaves and foreigners were excluded from being citizens and from contributing to political decision making in these contexts. But when Jesus proclaimed, "I will build my *ekklesia*" (Matt 16:18), this new creation included the powerful and the weak, the insiders and the outcasts, slaves, women, and the poor. A term used for exclusion became a radical expression of inclusion. And it subversively confronted the empire's political systems, because Jesus, not the town clerk, called this *ekklesia* in order to conduct the affairs of the kingdom of God rather than merely the affairs of the empire. As Amos Yong writes, "These kinds of ecclesial communities by their very existence constitute a prophetic critique of the selfishness, injustice, and violence that characterize the fallen structures of this world as well as threaten to overthrow the world's way of doing business altogether."[4]

One can sense an oasis of the Spirit's creation when a community is shaped by a vision of the new *ekklesia* and gives primary loyalty to the Lordship of Jesus Christ. When a community responds holistically to the teaching and call of Jesus Christ so that all aspects of life are brought under Jesus' loving purposes, the signpost flashes out the message, "Here is where God's Spirit is at work. This is evidence that God reigns and God's kingdom is in our midst."[5] When one can say, "This community gathers at Jesus' call to seek his guidance for conducting all aspects of their lives," it is obvious that the living well of the Holy Spirit is its sustaining and life-giving source. When one's imagination is shaped by this truth, there is no aspect of life that may be seen as outside God's love and God's reign.

---

2. Kittel, *Theological Dictionary of the New Testament*, vol. 3, 513.

3. Brown, ed., *The New International Dictionary of New Testament Theology*, 291. For a discussion of whether New Testament writers intended an anti-imperialist understanding, see Van Kooten, "The 'Church of God' and Civic Assemblies of the Greek Cities in the Roman Empire."

4. Yong, *Who Is the Holy Spirit?*, 56.

5. Cf. Wright: "The whole point of the gospels is to tell the story of how God became king, on earth as in heaven." *How God Became King*, 34.

Koinonia

A second shift in the mind and imagination of the people of the early church can be seen through the transformed meaning of the term *koinonia*. In Greco-Roman society it was a term describing common interest groups or partnerships, more like a contemporary club.[6] Such clubs were exclusive and created along lines of ethnicity, gender, and class. The church offered an iconoclastic contrast by being a *koinonia* that included Jew and Gentile, male and female, slave and free. This created an alternate image that was both attractive and scandalous. As Michael Green conveys in *Evangelism and the Early Church*, one of the most decisive contributors to growth of the church was the attractiveness of this radical inclusivity. "The Church had qualities unparalleled in the ancient world. Nowhere else would you find slaves and masters, Jews and Gentiles, rich and poor, engaging in table fellowship and showing a real love for one another. That love overflowed to outsiders."[7] No one could mistake the *koinonia* of the church for a *koinonia* of Rome.

Our *koinonia* points to the renewing waters of the Spirit, and is evident when communities of the church live by the awareness that this is no "social club" that we join through our own qualifications. All have been qualified by Christ and in Christ. All are welcome members of God's communion to share joyously in life together. This *koinonia* has one Master who invites all participants to feast with him at the table and to share with him by the Spirit in his prayers, praises, and celebration of God's grace. It might appear that the members are intoxicated with the new wine flowing into them as part of the celebration,[8] that they are foolish children caught up in joy and laughter, naïve about the grave issues of the world. It might be threatening to powers that work to control through fear and intimidation. But these members of Christ's *koinonia* can laugh and rejoice, because their intoxication comes from the Spirit of God who fills them with joy and who reassures them that all will be well. They may take themselves less seriously for their imaginations are filled with the radiance of God's reigning glory and thus more able to resist the shadows of fear.

6. See, for example, the fishing partnership between Peter, James, and John described as koinonia in Luke 5:10.

7. M. Green, *Evangelism and the Early Church*, 20.

8. See Acts 2:13.

Sacramentum

A third radical transformation of a culturally excluding term is evident in the term "sacrament." The early church took a common word that signified a soldier's oath of loyalty to Caesar, *sacramentum*, which evoked images of power and cultural divisions, and applied it to the central acts of radical inclusivity for followers of Jesus.[9] A sacred oath taken to crush all opposition to the lordship of Caesar is confronted by a sacred oath offered by Jesus to the Father on our behalf to liberate people from all oppressive powers. This contrasting expression of devotion to God rather than Caesar becomes a life-giving fountain for us, in which we are made new and empowered to freely pledge our participation in Jesus' life. Thus, early believers took a word that evoked images of Roman dominance and control and linked it instead with Jesus, who gave up power and pledged loyalty to us through his baptism on the cross, and his own body and blood shared with us. "Sacrament" now evoked visions of Jesus' dying and rising, and our participation in that dying and rising, such that all other loyalties and identities are placed at Jesus' feet. What formerly stimulated images of Roman repression, now is meant to catalyze images of inclusivity and egalitarian participation in Christ's new life, in which all die, all rise, and all become new creatures in Christ who are together fed by his own body.

Thus, when a community welcomes people as those to whom Jesus has bound himself, whether Jew or Gentile, slave or free, male or female, Scythian or Barbarian, one can sense this is no mirage. This is an oasis of God's sacramental community, drinking deeply from the well of the Holy Spirit's new creation. This is a community that has allowed the Spirit to transform their imaginations so they see themselves now as one family, one body, no longer separated by secondary identity markers of gender, ethnicity, or class. Here is a community that welcomes all people because it exists in humble response to the central sacred oath that God has taken in Christ toward us. It recognizes that our sacred oaths are merely a participation in Christ's oath given in our humanity and on our behalf in response to the Father's love. Christ was baptized for us and with us. Christ offers his body and blood as our sustenance. Our enactments of baptism and communion may vary, but they are all united in the central sacrament of God in Christ given for us, and it is by the Holy Spirit that we may share in Christ's

9. The first Christian reference to the adaptation of the term *sacramentum* was by Tertullian in the late second century. Tertullian, *De baptismo* IV.4–5, as cited in Van Slyke, "The Changing Meanings of *sacramentum*," 252.

sacrament. If the central sacred oath is given by God in Christ, that Word trumps all our words of response, and draws them into a unity in the Spirit, such that Paul could say there is "one body and one Spirit . . . one Lord, one faith, one baptism, one God and Father of all, who is above all and through all and in all" (Eph 4:4–6).

In these ways, *ekklesia, koinonia,* and *sacramentum* became new icons of kingdom life and signposts of the work of the Holy Spirit. They enabled and catalyzed a reimagining of the purpose and meaning of life.

Historical Oases

Throughout history where these signposts have been evident, even though marred and somewhat defaced, the world has experienced an oasis of God's kingdom, and the church has lived into its deeper identity as a reconciled and reconciling people. Though there are many such oases evident through-out church history, I want briefly to highlight four that stand out. They remind us today what is possible when God's Spirit is allowed to recreate our imaginations and transform us into the new ecclesia and koinonia, and to fill us with the life and wine of the new sacrament.

Early Church

The birth of the early church is powerful evidence of God's intentions for new creation. It is the embodiment of the new ecclesia and koinonia, and the great evidence of God's sacred oath to the world. We have explored the impact of the Holy Spirit transforming the imaginations and lives of Peter and Paul, specifically. More broadly, a vision of the impact of the Spirit on the larger community is evident in Acts 2. It was after the calamity of Jesus' death, the joyous triumph of his resurrection, and a season of "constantly devoting themselves to prayer" that their lives and imaginations were flooded with power from on high (Acts 1:14—2:4).

As the Holy Spirit was poured out on all flesh and as people welcomed this new life, entire communities were so taken with this new vision, new hope, and new love that walls came down and people could see they were all part of one family, under one loving Lord, sharing in one glorious king-dom. People were considered both drunk and dangerous. Yet their joy and fearlessness drew in others by the thousands to drink of this new living water, and to join this koinonia. A vision of a Lord who loved them and had given everything for them freed them to make all that they owned available for the needs and purposes of this *ekklesia*. And the Spirit was able to work through them in ways that they had previously been unable to imagine. "Awe came upon everyone, because many wonders and signs were being done by the apostles. All who believed were together and had all things in common; they would sell their possessions and goods and distribute the proceeds to all, as any had need. Day by day, as they spent much time together in the temple, they broke bread at home and ate their food with glad and generous hearts, praising God and having the goodwill of all the people. And day by day the Lord added to their number those who were being saved" (Acts 2:43–47).

The re-creating presence of the Holy Spirit not only came with power, generous hearts, and liberating unity, but also fostered immense creativity. Disciples were given dreams and visions, hymns of joy and thanksgiving, and wisdom of speech that astounded the authorities. And a radical community was created such that Paul could embrace a slave as a brother, honor women in the roles of apostle, deacon, teacher, and coworker, and reach out to the poor and rich alike.[10] Curtiss DeYoung writes, "First-century congregations established new revolutionary reconciliation structures for colonized and colonizers, women and men, marginalized and privileged, to rediscover their true identity in Christ and live into the full realization of what it meant to be one humanity."[11]

Paul describes the gifts of the Spirit as available to all without any needed qualifications related to gender, ethnicity, or class. They had all been qualified already in Christ, and cleansed by his life, death, and resurrection so the "earthen vessel" in which the treasure lived was no longer a limit but now could be envisioned as a wonder (2 Cor 4:7). It was now a rich reminder that God's strength is made perfect in weakness, and that God's process had always been to place God's treasure in the least likely, rather than the most likely, earthen vessels.[12]

---

10. See the Letter to Philemon on Onesimus, a former slave; Romans 16:1 for Paul's extolling "our sister Phoebe, a deacon"; Rom 16:7, "Junia . . . prominent among the apostles"; Romans 16:34; and Philippians 4:2–3 on women as Paul's coworkers; and Acts 18:27 on Priscilla as a teacher.

11. Boesak and DeYoung, *Radical Reconciliation*, 85.

12. See, for example, the biblical leaders Jacob, Joseph, Moses, Ruth, Esther, David, Daniel. Also, see Jesus' statement, "At that same hour Jesus rejoiced in the Holy Spirit and said, 'I thank you, Father, Lord of heaven and earth, because you have hidden these things from the wise and the intelligent and have revealed them to infants; yes, Father,

As Amos Yong writes, "How is it that these early disciples were able to break free from the class-divided and hierarchically ordered imperial structure and live with one another as equals? Perhaps this had something to do with the life and teachings of the one they followed. Perhaps they had indeed been empowered by the Spirit to restore the kingdom to Israel and did so by bringing down the mighty and lifting up the lowly . . . and by proclaiming release to the captives and freedom to those who were oppressed ([Acts] 4:18)."[13]

Celtic Christian Faith[14]

The second oasis I want to profile briefly is the Celtic Christian movement, as further evidence of what happens to Christian communities that more fully honor the power and presence of the Holy Spirit. "Celtic cultures survived predominantly in regions that escaped the rule of Rome, thus in Northern Scotland, Wales, Ireland and parts of England. Celtic forms of Christianity are usually associated with particular traditions in these parts of the British Isles, evident between the 5th and 12th centuries."[15] Though not a monolithic movement, its various expressions convey the signposts of ecclesia, koinonia, and sacrament that were described earlier. And though many would like to dismiss Celtic Christianity to be as mythical as the legends of King Arthur, the lingering impact of these oases can still be felt today.[16]

Celtic Christian expressions can be traced to early Eastern leaders, who honored the Trinitarian nature of the faith, including emphasis on the Holy Spirit. "Eastern Orthodoxy penetrated into Celtic life through a variety of means. Eastern Christian churches of Asia Minor and leaders like Irenaeus and St. Anthony are noted as early influences on Celtic

---

for such was your gracious will'" (Luke 10:21). See also Paul's description of those whom God has chosen as recipients of God's truth in 1 Corinthians 1:26–31.

13. Yong, *Who Is the Holy Spirit?*, 56.

14. Much of the material in this section comes from Dearborn, "Recovering a Trinitarian and Sacramental Ecclesiology," 39–73.

15. Ibid., 30.

16. For example, egalitarian, celebrative, and creation-care elements of Celtic Christianity still mark Scottish culture in very distinctive ways. Specific evidence of those marks include long-standing access to education across economic lines, Ceilidh dances that include people from every part of a community, accessible and quality health care for all, and resistance to materialism.

Christians."[17] Athanasius depicts Anthony as possessing many gifts of the Spirit, including the discernment of spirits, healing for the sick, and deliverance for the demonized.[18] Celtic Christians developed their openness to the Spirit's gifts and presence and their devotion to monastic life in part through the inspiration of the father of monasticism, Anthony, who appears on numerous Celtic crosses in Ireland.[19]

Celtic Ecclesia

The signpost of ecclesia was evident in Celtic Christianity through its holistic way of approaching all things as under the Lordship of Jesus Christ, and all aspects of life as ways to share in God's purposes. This oasis of Christian expression included and honored all people in a given region, such that issues of gender, class, and ethnicity did not preclude people from having a voice in how the affairs of the community were conducted. All types of work were honored as ways through which God could be served and worshiped, so prayers were written to express praise to God when rekindling the fire in the morning, dressing, farming, and eating.[20] "The spirituality of ordinary lay people was a monastic spirituality . . . which means . . . essentially to follow a liturgical life shaped by a regular, ordered rhythm—yearly, seasonal, daily."[21]

Belief that the One who called them to conduct the affairs of the kingdom was actually with them and enfolding them as Father, Son, and Spirit kept them from dividing life into sacred and secular realms. Spiritual and material, heaven and earth were seen as so interpenetrating that Celts embraced a unique sense of time. Eternity was always present in some way and invited people's awareness, gratitude, and praise. Time itself was seen as God's creation and gift, so that ordinary moments could share in the rhythms of God's reign.[22]

Rigorous disciplines were practiced to bring all aspects of life into harmony with God's triune life and purposes. Holiness was embraced as flowing from salvation, which was seen as being united with God in Christ

17. Joyce, *Celtic Christianity*, 23–24.

18. Athanasius, *Life of Anthony*, 11–12, 94.

19. De Waal, *Celtic Way of Prayer*, 94.

20. De Waal, *Celtic Vision*, 36.

21. De Waal, *Celtic Way of Prayer*, 52–53.

22. Sellner, *Wisdom*, 25.

and sharing by the Spirit in the life of the Trinity. "The emphasis was not on 'sin-management' so common in the Western church, but on essential transformation to become more like Christ.[23] Thus all were invited to live the life of a monk, even those who were married with children."[24]

Celtic Koinonia

The second signpost of koinonia was reflected in the Celts' egalitarian approach to community life, in which God alone is the one who owns all things. As in Acts 2, Celtic communities held things in common. "As John Ó Ríordáin notes: 'there is no word in the Irish language for 'private property' and there is no verb 'to possess.' The term for one's property is *mo chuid*—my portion; the underlying social and legal position being that the wealth of the community was owned by the community and out of that resource each got enough to live on.'"[25] In describing koinonia, DeYoung points out that, "true community is possible only when there is sacrifice and substantial sharing."[26]

The koinonia signpost was also evident in Celtic Christianity through their egalitarian approach to women and their treatment of strangers, though admittedly not in their approach to rival Celtic tribes. Celts are known for their interclan battles, both before and after becoming Christianized, though the gospel did make them less ferocious than before.[27]

Even so, there was a deep recognition that the Spirit of God does speak through people, regardless of background, ethnicity, or gender.[28] Thus, women as well as men could bear God's good news to the community of faithful and to those yet to hear of the evangel.[29] Jones asserts, "It was a

23. For a helpful discussion of "sin-management," see Willard, *Divine Conspiracy*, 35–59.

24. Dearborn, "Recovering a Trinitarian and Sacramental Ecclesiology," 35.

25. Ibid., 38, with reference to Ó Ríordáin, *The Music of What Happens*, 69, in Jones, *With an Eagle's Eye*, 95.

26. DeYoung, *Coming Together in the 21st Century*, 157.

27. Graydon Snyder asserts, "The Jesus tradition, with its rejection of violence, filtered out Celtic ferocity. This is not to say that fighting departed from the Irish soil. Surely there continued to be quarrels among the tuath. But the *Vitae* and the traditions do not reflect Irish ferocity. Tenacity, yes, ferocity, no." *Irish Jesus, Roman Jesus*, 206.

28. Mackey, ed., *An Introduction*, 15–16, 50.

29. As mentioned previously, egalitarian views of men and women were also part of the legacy of pre-Christian Celtic culture and were sustained by their later nonhierarchical

community of equals."[30] Both men and women offered leadership in education, pastoral care, and liturgical matters, and both women and men in turn would help the leaders "to grow their crops, manage their farms, fish, plant trees and keep their bees."[31] Women and men were given similar legal rights, and women could hold "powerful ecclesial positions in communities consisting of both women and men."[32]

This resonates with Moltmann's assertion, conveyed in *The Source of Life*: "In the fellowship of the Holy Spirit, men and women are charismatically commissioned and endowed to preach the gospel. . . . The ordination of women is not a matter of adaptation to changed social conditions. It has to do with new life from the beginnings of the Christian church: life out of the fellowship of the Holy Spirit."[33]

Celtic Sacrament

For Celtic Christians all parts of life were seen in sacramental ways, as God's gracious offering and as signs of God's redeeming presence. Because of this awareness, the stranger, the earth, and the arts were honored as means of experiencing Christ, who had not only created all things but had bound himself to the very physicality of our lives. The stranger was to be honored because in each person the sacramental presence of Christ waited to be discovered.[34] As David Adam writes, "The Celtic Christians did not so much seek to bring Christ as to discover him; not to possess him, but to see him in 'friend and stranger'; to liberate the Christ who is already there in all his riches."[35] Followers of Christ were called to be hospitable as a way of sharing in God's sacramental self-offering to draw others into triune communion and love. That meant both going out to extend God's love and mercy to the world, and also welcoming others in. "*Peregrini* were not sent out so much to conquer as to invite people into the glorious feast of faith that God has provided for all people.[36] Since they viewed mission as the

understanding of the Trinity. Cf. Joyce, *Celtic Christianity*, 17.

30. Jones, *With an Eagle's Eye*, 57.

31. Sellner, *Wisdom*, 18.

32. Dearborn, "Recovering a Trinitarian and Sacramental Ecclesiology," 37.

33. Moltmann, *Source of Life*, 101–2.

34. Jones, *With an Eagle's Eye*, 29.

35. Adam, *The Cry of the Deer*, 28.

36. Cf. Jones: "Celtic monks had a compulsion to share the joy of their consciousness

work of the Holy Spirit, they approached their participation in that work with both passion and humility."[37]

Creation was viewed as part of God's sacrament of love to the world.[38] "Creation was ennobled first by having been created by a loving Father, who proclaimed it good. Second, creation was seen as blessed in being able to host the divine. The reality of the Incarnation as God with us, the eternal Word made flesh, was understood as God's affirmation of the material world, which was drawn with humanity into the process of re-creation in Jesus' life and death. Third, the presence of the triune God through the Holy Spirit in Christ and through Christ to the world, was seen as the way in which God continues to penetrate and consecrate the earthly domain to bring God's healing and restoration."[39]

Celtic Christians also honored the imagination and thus "the arts . . . could be a fount from which truth could flow to refresh and challenge both seekers and believers."[40] Celtic Christians were called "God-intoxicated people" who relished all of life and who believed the incarnation gives value to what is sensual, human, and of the material order.[41]

Enduring Celtic Christian wellsprings of Christian faith and arts are evident in the writings of George MacDonald, C. S. Lewis, and J. R. R. Tolkien. "For MacDonald that included the Celtic or Gaelic influences of Scotland. For Lewis it came through Irish Celtic thought and for Tolkien through his love and knowledge of the Welsh language. Though Tolkien at one early point denied Celtic influence in his writing of [The] Silmarillion, later in his letters he acknowledged Celtic influences in his creation of the Elves and their language."[42] Each of these authors offers a sacramental view of life, challenges tribalistic approaches to the "other," and offers visions of life lived in harmony with God and others that have provided refresh-

---

of the Holy Three and of God's creation." *With an Eagle's Eye*, 58.

37. Dearborn, "Recovering a Trinitarian and Sacramental Ecclesiology," 51.

38. For further reading on Celtic sacramental belief see Jones, *With an Eagle's Eye*, 21–22; Mackey, ed., *An Introduction*, viii, 18, 50; De Waal, *Celtic Vision*, xxx–xxxii; Sellner, *Wisdom*, 21–22.

39. Dearborn, "Recovering a Trinitarian and Sacramental Ecclesiology," 45.

40. Ibid., 46.

41. Furthermore, the corporate nature of Celtic spirituality emphasized belonging and relationships, which tended to prevent "any inward journey from becoming one of interior self-exploration." De Waal, *Celtic Way of Prayer*, 26.

42. Dearborn, "The Sacrament of the Stranger," 298. See also Fimi, "'Mad' Elves and 'Elusive Beauty,'" 156–70.

ment, hope, and inspiration for many people.[43] They have expanded our imagination to perceive the wonder of God's reconciliation of all things in Christ, and our confidence that God's healing, humble, and gracious ways ultimately triumph. Thus, many people, both Christian and non-Christian continue to drink from these springs of new life.

Wesleyan

The Wesleyan revival took seriously the presence of God through the Holy Spirit. Thus it also created an oasis of life drawing people to God's living water, overcoming barriers and fostering holistic, transformative, creative approaches to life. As with the Spirit working dramatically in Peter and Cornelius's lives in Acts 10, for Wesley the Spirit's powerful anointing came after a long season of prayer and desperation for more of God in his life. Wesley describes in his *Journal* this deeper encounter with Holy Spirit, which came in the midst of a time of praying through the night: "At about three in the morning, as we were continuing instant in prayer, the power of God came mightily upon us insomuch that many cried out for exceeding joy, and many fell to the ground. . . . We broke out with one voice, 'We praise thee, O God, we acknowledge thee to be the Lord.'"[44] Their responsiveness to the Holy Spirit not only ushered in occasional gifts of healing and laughter, but also a deep sense of assurance and the nurturing of communities that expressed ecclesia, koinonia, and sacramental signposts.[45]

Wesleyan Ecclesia and Sacrament

Similar to the early church, Wesley viewed Christian faith holistically as shaping all aspects of life with the recognition that all things are under God's authority and grace. Early in his life, John Wesley wrote in his diary, "Instantly I resolved to dedicate *all my life* to God, *all* my thoughts, and

---

43. For more information on these themes in MacDonald, Lewis, and Tolkien, see Dearborn, "The Sacrament of the Stranger," 297–303.

44. Wesley, *Journal*, Jan. 1, 1739.

45. Hyatt, *2000 Years of Charismatic Christianity*, 102–4. Randy Maddox clarifies that Wesley "affirmed both divine and medical healing," and though there were relatively few descriptions of solely divine healing, Wesley urged people to see God as the Great Physician, "who wants to give you . . . both inward and outward health." Maddox, "John Wesley on Holistic Health and Healing," 7, 10.

words, and actions; being thoroughly convinced, there was no medium; but that *every part* of my life (not *some* only) must either be a sacrifice to God, or myself, that is, in effect, to the devil."[46]

As Deborah Madden affirms, "Wesley's holistic understanding of salvation took him, in fact, to the very heart of human anguish. He spoke out against slavery, campaigned for prison reform and gave alms—as well as medicines—to the poor. . . . Wesley's concept of nature and the environment, which underpinned his active participation in medical science, sprang from this holistic framework of holy living, but also . . . of holy dying."[47]

Affirming the intersection of visible and invisible realms of existence, as well as the interconnectedness of body and soul, Wesley advocated healing prayer as well as the latest medical approaches to the treatment of the sick.[48] He was hopeful that both physical and spiritual healing could be experienced in the present, not merely at the resurrection, and that approaches to health care would be more "balanced and integrative."[49]

Furthermore, Wesley took seriously God's concern and love for all of creation, and in contrast to the deists of his day, insisted that "God actively participates in sustaining the creation."[50] Not only is God present, sustaining creation, but also God in Christ has made possible the new creation, which beckons us into a dramatically different life now. Wesley writes, "There is a new creation—Only the power that makes a world can make a Christian. . . . Behold—The present, visible, undeniable change! All things are become new—He has new life, new senses, new faculties, new affections, new appetites, new ideas and conceptions. . . . God, men, the whole creation, heaven, earth, and all therein appear in a new light, and stand related to him in a new manner, since he was created anew in Christ Jesus."[51] Wesley envisioned a restoration of all creation in which all organisms would live in harmony. "All of creation, degraded as a result of the Fall, would share in the final salvation of the new creation, the new earth."[52]

---

46. Wesley, *A Plain Account of Christian Perfection*, §2.

47. Madden, "Introduction: Saving Souls and Saving Lives," 9.

48. Ibid.

49. Maddox, "Reclaiming the Eccentric Parent," 17, 34.

50. Flowers, "Environmental Stewardship," 61.

51. Wesley, *Explanatory Notes on the New Testament*, 2 Cor 5:17, 657.

52. Flowers, "Environmental Stewardship," 73.

Wesley called Christians to treat all things as entrusted by God to us and thus to be cared for according to God's purposes.[53]

Thus, Wesley's conviction that God's mercy is over all his works led him to affirm a sacramental view of creation. He affirmed that God had given value to all parts of creation and intended for God's image bearers to extend that care to all birds and beasts, as well as all humans.[54] It was this hope in him through the Holy Spirit's anointing that empowered him to re-envision the Christian life not merely as the forgiven life but the transformed, reconciled, and reconciling life for his own generation and for generations to come. The sacraments of baptism and communion were considered means of grace by which one entered into that new life and could progress by the Spirit toward living more fully as the new creation. They were envisioned as ways through which our lives could be more fully united with the life of Christ and transformed by the Holy Spirit.

Wesleyan Koinonia

Wesley's profound experience of the Holy Spirit catalyzed him to preach the gospel joyfully wherever he could. Rejected by members of his own church as an "enthusiast," Wesley began preaching in the open air. His first open-air sermon was based on Luke 4:18–19: "The Spirit of the Lord is upon Me, because he has anointed me to preach good news to the poor . . ."[55] The Wesleyan revival began as an anointing by the Holy Spirit to love society's marginalized and came to reflect an inclusive approach of extending the love of God to all people. Power came through their ministry for healing, exorcism, and reaching out to many disheartened people who yearned for hope and new life.[56] Wesley recounts one evening in which "our Lord rose on many who were wounded, 'with healing in his wings.'"[57] As in the early church, some described their gatherings as "more like a drunken

---

53. See Wesley, "The General Deliverance" and "The New Creation."

54. Flowers, "Environmental Stewardship," 75. See also Wesley, "The General Deliverance."

55. Wesley, *Journal*, April 2, 1739, *Works*, 19:46. See also Tomkins, *John Wesley*, 72–73.

56. Wesley, *Journal*, Oct. 12–23, 1739, *Works*, 19:104–110.

57. Ibid., 104. See also Wesley, *The Principles of a Methodist, further explained*, IV.10, *Works*, 9:211.

rabble than the worshippers of God" and others thought of them as fools.[58] But creativity flourished through John Wesley's sermons and essays, and through his brother Charles's hymns, which began to pour forth almost daily, reaching nearly 9,000 in number by Charles's death. The first official meeting place of the London Methodist Society, the Foundery, reflected their holistic approach, for it included "a meeting hall, school, and social welfare center."[59]

The inclusive nature of Wesleyan koinonia was reflected in three ways: honoring the gifts of lay preachers, honoring the voices and wisdom of women, and resistance to slave trade and ownership. Though Wesley incurred deep criticism for allowing people who were not ordained to preach and teach, he sensed God's gifting in their lives and knew it would be helpful for the expansion of God's work.[60] This laid the foundation for later Methodist success "among African Americans in the eighteenth century . . . for their openness in authorizing blacks to preach. Black Methodist clergy, sometimes in cooperation with white colleagues and at other times alone, proved effective in attracting African Americans, both slave and free, to the Wesleyan fold."[61]

Wesley allowed women to use their teaching and leadership gifts. "Wesley had from the start given women more responsibility and authority than they had ever had in the Church of England, appointing them as leaders of bands and classes and he encouraged them as much as men to spread the gospel among their personal acquaintances."[62] Though he developed unofficial rules to limit women's full equality with men in preaching and leadership, he allowed women to "preach," as part of the "extraordinary movements of the Spirit."[63] Wesley was influenced by biblical affirmations that both male and female are created in God's image (Gen 5:2), and that both sons and daughters prophesied by the power of the Holy Spirit in Acts 2:17.[64] Paul's inclusive statement in Galatians 3:28 also shaped his thinking. "Herein there is no difference, 'there is neither male nor female in Christ

---

58. Crowder, *New Mystics,* 276–77.

59. Liardon, *God's Generals,* 66.

60. Tomkins, *John Wesley,* 81–82.

61. Dickerson, "The African-American Wing of the Wesleyan Tradition," 283.

62. Tomkins, *John Wesley,* 159.

63. Maddox, "'Honoring Conference,'" 94.

64. Ibid., 92–93.

Jesus.'"[65] It is difficult to point to John Wesley as an unambiguous example of reconciled relationships with women when he had such a troubled relationship with his own wife. But he clearly had women ministering alongside of him, and recognized their gifts and abilities, which was remarkable for the context.

Specific examples of Wesley's campaign against slavery are evident in his pamphlet, *Thoughts upon Slavery*, and in the last letter he wrote, which was to William Wilberforce, encouraging him in his crusade against slavery.[66] Wesley's holistic and inclusive understanding of faith fostered "emphasis on the spiritual and corporal dignity of every man" and a yearning to "seek out and minister to the forgotten people of Britain."[67] Thus John and Charles Wesley established medical clinics for the poor in London, and cared for those in workhouses.[68]

Through Wesley's experiences, teaching, and writing, the foundation was laid for openness to the Holy Spirit among Christians that would flow to future generations and spread to all parts of the globe. Vinson Synan, a Pentecostal historian, credits John Wesley and the emerging Methodist church as being a major influence on what would become the Pentecostal movement.[69] Wesley was willing to challenge understandings of church history that, first, justified the church's criticism of those who experienced the miraculous gifts of the Spirit, and second, taught that these gifts were no longer necessary. Addressing the first, he wrote in his journal for August 15, 1750, "I was fully convinced of what I had long suspected, (1) That the Montanists, in the second and third centuries, were real, scriptural Christians; and, (2) that the grand reason why the miraculous gifts were so soon withdrawn was not only that faith and holiness were well nighlost; but that dry, formal, orthodox men began even then to ridicule whatever gifts they had not themselves, and to decry them all as either madness or imposture."[70]

---

65. Wesley, "On Visiting the Sick," 396.

66. Wesley, *Thoughts upon Slavery*, 11:59–79; and Wesley's "Letter to Wilberforce," 13:153.

67. Liardon, *God's Generals*, 74.

68. See the discussion of these various ministries in Marquardt, *John Wesley's Social Ethics*.

69. See Synan, *The Holiness-Pentecostal Tradition*.

70. Wesley, *Journal*, Aug. 15, 1750, *Works*, 20:356–57.

Wesley brought together numerous historical and biblical arguments to address the second criticism, that the miraculous gifts of the Spirit were no longer needed. He referred to Paul's teaching on gifts in 1 Corinthians 12, and expressed his interpretation for why they had ceased to be very prominent. Wesley writes about the decline of spiritual gifts following Constantine, saying, "The cause of this was not (as has been vulgarly supposed,) 'because there was no more occasion for them' because all the world was become Christian. . . . The real cause was, 'the love of many,' almost of all Christians, so called, was 'waxed cold.'"[71] It was often through the image-rich forms of Wesleyan music and worship, and their close koinonia, that the embers of love were fanned once again into a flame of passion and devotion.

In these ways the oasis of God's renewing and transformative life that emerged from the Wesleyan revival was able to reveal the abundance of the underground streams of God's living water and prepare the way for today's global movement of Pentecostalism connected with the Azusa Street Revival. Thus Pentecostal historian Synan writes, "Perhaps the most important immediate precursor to Pentecostalism was the Holiness movement which issued from the heart of Methodism at the end of the Nineteenth Century. From John Wesley, the Pentecostals inherited the idea of a subsequent crisis experience variously called 'entire sanctification,' 'perfect love,' 'Christian perfection,' or 'heart purity.'"[72]

Azusa Street Revival

The multiracial, multiethnic, multinational nature of today's Pentecostal movement is often traced back to the son of former slaves (William Seymour), the niece of Frederick Douglass (Lucy Farrow), and a dilapidated building, formerly a Methodist church, in Los Angeles. As Harvey Cox writes, "Pentecostalism has become a global vehicle for the restoration of primal hope. The movement started from the bottom. A partially blind, poor, black man with little or no book learning outside of the Bible heard a call. Seymour was anything but a Paul of Tarsus . . . or an Augustine . . . or a Calvin or Luther. . . . He was a son of former slaves who had to listen to sermons through a window and who undoubtedly traveled to Los Angeles in the segregated section of the train. Yet under Seymour's guidance,

71. Wesley, "The More Excellent Way," Sermon 89, §2, *Works*, 3:263–64

72. Synan, "The Origins of the Pentecostal Movement."

a movement arose whose impact on Christianity . . . has been compared to the Protestant Reformation."[73]

Though "no main personality can be said to be the originator of the movement" and though it was not centered in one place, as Cox mentioned one of the key focal points was William Seymour and Azusa Street.[74] The Holy Spirit touched William Seymour early in his life, such that he "experienced divine visions" and "taught himself to read by constantly reading the Bible."[75] At a time when people questioned whether blacks even had a soul and Jim Crow laws restricted access to education, Seymour claimed his identity in Christ and the invitation to biblical training from God. Thus he was not deterred by Charles Parham's reluctance to let him attend Bible school in Topeka, Kansas because of the Jim Crow laws. He would "sit outside the window and listen, and on rainy days he could sit in the hallway where they would leave the classroom door open. And because of his race, Seymour was not allowed to 'tarry' at the altar seeking the Holy Spirit with the other white students."[76] From early on, Seymour evidenced the Holy Spirit's gift of a biblical imagination, through which he could see himself and his calling in God's light rather than merely in the disempowering quagmire of his context. He was able to hold the tension of the dehumanizing realities that surrounded him with a vision of God reaching out to him through Scripture and visions, and having created him to be a beloved son to share in God's own kingdom work.

In 1906 Seymour responded to a call to move to Los Angeles and persisted in his ministry there despite criticisms of his theology and being locked out of the church that had called him to preach. He humbly began to organize prayer meetings in the homes of black friends. In response to the arrival of Lucy Farrow, a Pentecostal preacher from Houston, he called for ten days of prayer and fasting. Thus, as with the disciples in Acts 2, Peter and Cornelius in Acts 10, and Wesley, prayer became the means by which the living water was drawn up to create another oasis of God's reign on earth. People felt the power of God's presence, were healed, spoke in tongues, and "for three days they celebrated 'early Pentecost restored.'"[77] So many people were drawn to this home that Seymour used the front porch

73. Cox, *Fire from Heaven*, 119.

74. McClung, *Azusa Street and Beyond*, 4.

75. Liardon, *Azusa Street Revival*, 89.

76. Ibid., 92.

77. Ibid., 97.

of the house as his pulpit until it collapsed, and they were forced to find another venue, the former Methodist church on Azusa Street.

Pentecostal Koinonia

Again one of the primary signs of God's reign was evident in the inclusiveness of their koinonia, the breaking down of the dividing walls between genders, races, classes, and even ages—the ability to reimagine one another in the light of God's love and presence above all. An evangelist named Frank Bartleman, who attended the meetings, wrote, "Every fresh division or party in the church gives to the world a contradiction as to the oneness of the body of Christ, and the truthfulness of the Gospel. Multitudes are bowing down and burning incense to a doctrine rather than Christ. . . . The Spirit is laboring for the unity of believers today, for the 'one body,' that the prayer of Jesus may be answered, 'that they all may be one, that the world may believe.'"[78]

Bartleman went on to describe the egalitarian nature of the gatherings:

> We wanted to hear from God, through whomever He might speak. We had no respect of persons. All were equal. . . . These were Holy Spirit meetings, led of the Lord. It had to start in poor surroundings to keep out the selfish, human element. . . . In honor we "preferred one another." The Lord was liable to burst through anyone. We prayed for this continually. Someone would finally get up, anointed for the message. All seemed to recognize this and gave way. It might be a child, a woman, or a man. It might be from the back seat or from the front. It made no difference. We rejoiced that God was working. . . . The whole place was steeped in prayer. . . . I have stopped more than once within two blocks of the place and prayed for strength before I dared go on. The presence of the Lord was so real.[79]

The multiracial, multiethnic, gender-inclusive, and ecumenical nature of this revival correlates with previous renewal movements in the Holy Spirit and is one of the reasons given that the movement spread so quickly, in addition to people gaining a new vision of what was possible in Christian faith both in one's experience of God and one's ministry flowing from God.[80]

78. Bartleman, *Azusa Street*, 127.

79. Ibid., 56–58.

80. McClung, *Azusa Street and Beyond*, 5. On the same page McClung notes that

The Apostolic Faith newspaper's first issue describes the rich diversity of the Azusa Street Revival. "God makes no difference in nationality. Ethiopians, Chinese, Indians, Mexicans, and other nationalities worship together."[81] There was a sense that all belonged together in the one body of Christ Jesus regardless of "color, dress, or lack of education."[82] The November issue of *The Apostolic Faith* affirmed this: "There is not Jew or Gentile, bond or free, in the Azusa Mission. No instrument that God can use is rejected on account of color or dress or lack of education. This is why God has built up the world. . . . The sweetest thing is the loving harmony."[83] There was a clear sense of heaven invading earth.

Yet negative reactions to this movement were swift and fierce, and the multiracial cohesion was fragile. Criticism of the movement focused on the multiracial nature of these gatherings as well as on unusual spiritual manifestations. One Los Angeles newspaper reported, "Disgraceful intermingling of the races, they cry and make howling noises all day and into the night. . . . They claim to be filled with the spirit. They have a one-eyed, illiterate, Negro as their preacher . . . supposed to be running the thing."[84] Opposition was so strong that worshipers were "cursed, jailed and physically assaulted."[85] Even Seymour's former mentor, Parham, when he visited was disturbed by the intensity, interclass, mixed-gender, and interracial makeup of the meetings.[86] By the end of 1906, the movement that had begun in such harmony and inclusivity was fracturing over issues of race, theological differences, and struggles for power. For example, as Daniel Castelo writes, "A falling out occurred between the leadership and the Mexican constituency of the mission so that the latter left around 1909."[87]

Rather than coming to a halt, though, the movement only sputtered for a time. Abundia (who was ordained by Seymour) and Rosa de Lopez extended the movement to the Mexican Plaza District of Los Angeles and

people in this movement embraced a new vision of God in their midst, empowering supernatural experiences and ministries reaching out to others to express to them God's healing presence and power. It also included a "tremendous spirit of sacrifice" and "a sense of belonging in community."

81. Liardon, *Azusa Street Revival*, 103.

82. Ibid.

83. Ibid., 104.

84. Martin, *The Life and Ministry of William J. Seymour*, 248–49.

85. Ibid., 251.

86. Ibid., 269.

87. Castelo, "Azusa Street Revival," 424.

beyond. Castelo writes that in spite of the rift in leadership, "The Pentecostal message was preached by and among Latinos/as throughout the borderlands and beyond by many who were linked in one way or another with Azusa."[88]

Similarly, evangelists like Lucy Farrow took their passion for God and Pentecostal anointing to other parts of the country and world. After being instrumental in the early days of the Azusa Street Revival, Farrow traveled to Norfolk, Virginia, via Houston and New Orleans. People were healed and experienced "their personal Pentecost" when she laid hands on them.[89] She spent from December 1906 to August 1907 in Liberia as an evangelist and healer, supported largely by people from the Azusa mission.

When asked what kept this Pentecostal movement going and contributed to its vigorous and rapid growth, missiologist Peter Wagner first credited God with the force behind it. Then he cited four additional factors: 1) churches of purity in belief in the Bible, Christian doctrine, and lifestyle; 2) churches of prayer; 3) churches of power; and 4) churches of the poor.[90]

In these factors, we again see evidence of the signposts of the Spirit's creative presence that emerge from long seasons of prayer, a renewed vision of God's presence and purposes touching all aspects of life, and a yearning for God to draw all people to God's living water. Thus, the poor were not excluded but were prioritized. Wagner explains:

> The God of the Bible is a God who loves the poor. It is true that He loves all people, including the rich; but if we take the Bible seriously, we know that He has a special bias for the poor. Because of this, God is going to make sure that the poor have a strong witness for Christ. Back in the eighteenth century, the Anglican Church in England had abandoned the poor, so God raised up the Methodist Church. When the Methodists came to America, they ministered to the poor with circuit riders going from cabin to cabin out on the frontier. But one hundred years later, the Methodists had become middle-class, and God raised up the Holiness/Pentecostal movement to minister to the poor once again. . . . Almost all Pentecostal preachers now in their sixties or seventies were born in poor homes, and many younger ones were also.[91]

88. Ibid.
89. Cauchi, "Lucy F. Farrow."
90. Wagner, " Characteristics of Pentecostal Church Growth," 127–30.
91. Ibid., 129.

The church was not formed by Christ to be like social clubs, divided along lines of race, class, gender, and ethnicity. Racial, economic, and gender inclusivity is a sign of the present and coming kingdom. Thus Cox writes, "In this context, the mixing of the races was not just an early equal opportunity program. It had a powerful archetypal significance as well. It presaged a new world in which both the outer and the inner division of humankind would be abolished, and it was the harbinger of one of the great surprises of the twentieth century."[92]

Cox highlights the dramatic and creative means by which God inspired this movement of renewal and reconciliation. "In retrospect we can also describe the revival as the principal point in Western history at which the pulsating energy of African American spirituality, wedded by years of suffering to the Christian promise of the Kingdom of God, leaped across the racial barrier and became fused with similar motifs in the spirituality of poor white people."[93] The dynamic creativity of the Holy Spirit is evident in birthing such koinonia as an oasis of God's present and coming reign, and in transforming people's imagination to be able to envision what is possible. As in the early church, it was the inclusive nature of the community that became such a compelling sign of God's power. Interracial fellowship was "precisely what enabled Pentecostalism to speak with such power to the twentieth century."[94] It has also worked to contravene the impact of Western individualism. Cox clarifies, "the Pentecostal wave has an irreducibly communal dimension. The Spirit descends on groups gathered in prayer. . . . More importantly, for the Pentecostals the purpose of the Spirit's visitation . . . is not to ravish the soul of the individual but to gather up and knit together the broken human family."[95] That is not to say that individuals do not gain a deep sense of God's love for them, but that the rich experience of God's love fuels a responsive love for God and for all whom God has created.

Pentecostal Ecclesia

The holistic emphasis of Pentecostalism is evident in the integration of body, soul, and spirit, and in the call for purity in all areas of life. The

92. Cox, *Fire from Heaven,* 100.

93. Ibid., 99.

94. Ibid., 100.

95. Ibid.

impetus to move beyond doctrine into action and transformed life was evident even in its inception. Thus Cox writes, "In early Pentecostal theology faith and spirituality would be primarily matters not of ritual and dogma but of action and behavior."[96] Clearly there have been noteworthy moral failures among key leaders. Even so, the movement kept its moorings in the holiness movement, in the commands of Scripture, and the belief that we are called to demonstrate the reality of God's kingdom by the power of the Holy Spirit in this present age. These moorings are what shaped the moral imagination of participants. One of the key contributions of Pentecostalism has been described as "the way in which their *lived reality* transcends the characteristically Protestant and evangelical *propositions*."[97]

Pentecostalism has also been holistic in according emotions, senses, and the body a more important place in worship. "Pentecostal services commonly accord a greater place to bodily activity and movement than [do] received forms of Catholic and Protestant worship."[98] God is not merely an idea to reflect on, but a living and loving Presence who wants to bless, touch, transform, heal, and empower. Senses become a means by which one can discern and express what God is saying and doing, by which one may diagnose "the spiritual through the physical; the senses are taken up into the process of 'picking up what is there.'"[99] Laying on of hands is an important tangible means by which one may convey the love of God to another person. The biblical connection between one's physical and spiritual being is honored, such that confession is seen as an important part of receiving physical healing. As the ecclesia of God, the movement initially saw itself involved in all aspects of life, including political dimensions. "Theirs was a social, indeed a political, vision that—at least in its birthplace on Azusa Street—included a dream of racial harmony as radical as Martin Luther King's."[100]

---

96. Ibid., 114.

97. Hollenweger, "Towards a Charismatic Theology," 10.

98. Ibid., 26.

99. Ibid.

100. Cox, *Fire from Heaven*, 121. There is not space to enter into an analysis of the ways in which Pentecostal eschatology has affected the willingness of Pentecostals to engage with issues of systemic injustice or to challenge totalitarian or oppressive regimes. That has been a significant challenge for some contemporary liberation theologians who have been drawn into the Pentecostal movement, who are trying to urge the movement to expand in these ways (e.g., Paul Alexander, Bob Ekblad).

Pentecostal Sacramentalism[101]

What empowered so much creativity, vibrancy, and dynamism among Pentecostals that would occasion such explosive growth around the world? In just one hundred years Pentecostalism has expanded to the point of including at least one fourth of the world's two billion Christians.[102] In many ways the growth can be linked to restoring hope to people who were marginalized, oppressed, and left by the side of the road to perish. As they felt the love of God impact them in tangible ways their imaginations were transformed to give them a vision of the greatness of God, their own worth, and of God's desire both to bless them and to bless others through them. The gifts of the Spirit were like sacred oaths of God's love bringing "good news to the poor . . . release to the captives and recovery of sight to the blind, to let the oppressed go free, to proclaim the year of the Lord's favor" (Luke 4:18–19). This included belief "in the sacramentality of speaking in tongues."[103] The *sacramentum* of God's blessing and love came alive when they sensed that they were being given God's own sacred words with which to pray and worship. "The Holy Spirit comes to free us from dumbness, restores our confidence to speak."[104] The sense of God inviting them into the new creation seemed palpable. "If it is in any sense true that man was created to speak God's language, then man must be the poet-priest of creation, uttering aloud the word by which God created each thing and all things in the silence of his heart."[105]

Because of God's redeeming love for us in Christ, Pentecostals affirm the possibility for all people to become sacramental vessels, filled with God's

101. As Castelo notes, "Historically, Pentecostals have tended not to be very self-consciously sacramental" but have "felt more at ease to talk about 'ordinances' rather than 'sacraments." *Revisioning Pentecostal Ethics*, 98. Yet a sacramental approach rooted in the person and life of Christ is evident. Castelo expounds, "If Christ is the true sacrament, then his body displays a kind of sacramental existence, not simply by its existence per se but more definitely and deeply by its evident shape and character." Thus, there is a willingness to broaden the sense of the sacramental to include actions such as foot washing. *Revisioning Pentecostal Ethics*, 50, 51. James K. A. Smith describes a Pentecostal approach to baptism that again suggests an expansive view of that sacrament: "Baptism in a Pentecostal church brings together the charismatic and the sacramental: their baptism is situated in a narrative enacted through song and sermon, echoed in the story of their testimonies as they present themselves for baptism." *Thinking in Tongues*, 106.

102. Pew Research Forum, "Pentecostal Resource Page."

103. Tugwell, "The Speech-Giving Spirit," 151.

104. Ibid., 138.

105. Ibid., 146.

love, and poured out for others. In the process of honoring God's ability to sanctify and speak through whomever God chooses, theology has also been transformed to include greater emphasis on the goodness, greatness, and love of God. As Cox acknowledges, "The salience of women in this movement has resulted in a dramatically different conception of who God is, and the quiet subversion of patriarchal theology."[106] In fact Cox asserts that one of the reasons the Pentecostal movement spread so quickly was because of empowerment and honoring of women.[107] Furthermore, Cox asserts, even as women were the "principal agents of its spread," music was "its principal medium."[108] Thus, this profound gift of the creative imagination, which was so central to the Wesleyan revival, was also vital to the Holy Spirit's renewal of people via the Pentecostal movement.

The sacramental vision of Pentecostals has given rise to a deepened sense of calibrating our lives according to the kingdom of God rather than the kingdoms of this world.[109] Tugwell writes, "The Pentecostal movement" embodies "not just a popular protest against the reigning assumptions of our time, but also an outline of an alternative, a heavenly city to replace the earthly one." He continues, "They succeeded because they brought hope to the losers whom the march of progress had left behind. They continue to evoke a response because they tell people who don't read sophisticated journals about a big change that is coming soon and in some ways already started."[110]

Concluding Reflections

Throughout this book we have explored the ways in which the Holy Spirit plays a central role in fulfilling God's work of reconciliation in Christ to bless and to draw all people into God's new creation. To ignore the work and presence of the Spirit is to clog up the springs of God's new creation with human efforts and human structures that ultimately fracture and

---

106. Ibid., 121.

107. Ibid.

108. Ibid.

109. For further helpful insights on Pentecostal sacramentalism see Castelo, *Revisioning Pentecostal Ethics,* and Chris E. W. Green's *Toward a Pentecostal Theology of the Lord's Supper.*

110. Tugwell, "The Speech-Giving Spirit," 117.

divide people rather than refresh and inspire us with the hope-filled vision that we have been made one in Christ.

I have also highlighted the ways in which our imagination is vital for the Holy Spirit's reconciling work in our world and lives. The Spirit baptizes and transforms the imagination so we can recognize the signs of God's work and drink deeply from the springs of new creation that would burst forth even in the most barren wildernesses. As we have seen, the Spirit often works in the very places and among the very people that to some may seem to be the lost causes of the world. As Jesus said, "The least among you all is the greatest" (Luke 9:48). Often it takes intense prayer and waiting on God to unclog those hidden springs of new life, so the Holy Spirit can work through the imagination to dissolve old fragmenting perspectives, recreate life-giving visions, and catalyze the kind of holistic loving community God created us for in the beginning. It may look unfamiliar and disturbing at times, as did all the renewal movements we briefly profiled. This is because it is the "new creation" and is ultimately "beyond all we can ask or even imagine" (Eph 3:20). Like the Pentecostal movement in Cox's description, the new creation represents, "a major reconfiguration of our most fundamental values and patterns of perception, one that will ultimately alter not just the way some people pray but the ways we all think, feel, work and govern."[111]

I would like to close this book with two specific examples of people who have drunk deeply from the renewing waters of the Holy Spirit, thus becoming a creative source of new vision and hope for others. One is Theresa Dedmon, a contemporary Christian leader in the Pentecostal movement, and the other, Harriet Beecher Stowe, has been a powerful inspiration for Dedmon and many others. Both have shared in God's new creation by the power of the Holy Spirit and have provided refreshing living water so people can taste the wonders of our reconciliation in Christ.

Theresa Dedmon is a pastor and an artist at Bethel Church in Redding, California. Her calling as a pastor is to catalyze Christians to use their creative gifts from God to nurture new life, healing, and transformation in businesses, banks, doctors' offices, and city streets. In her book *Born to Create* she describes the biblical foundation for taking more seriously the renewing gifts of the imagination as well as the impact on people when they welcome God's love and creativity into their lives and convey it freely to others.

111. Cox, *Fire from Heaven*, 120.

Her passion for churches to become vessels of blessing was awakened when she was thirteen. "My family and I would go to convalescent homes, veteran hospitals, prisons, orphanages, and city streets to touch people through music and drama. Everything inside me came alive as I saw people who felt sad, forgotten and broken know the love of a Father who would never leave them."[112] Now Dedmon is training hundreds of emerging leaders each year to open up more fully to God's love, to drink deeply of the Spirit's living water, and to be willing to risk in sharing it creatively with others.

Dedmon stirs up a feast of creativity through training people in Spirit-inspired painting, drama, culinary arts, music, writing, and dance. Prayer, attentiveness to God's Spirit, and openness to the new things that God would do have taken her and her students to partner with others around the world in awakening people to their identities in Christ as the Father's beloved children, and as colaborers with God by the power of the Holy Spirit. Because she has been given a profound vision of God's kingdom on earth and is gifted artistically, she not only sees but also imaginatively portrays the wonder of God's reconciling love for specific contexts and particular people's lives.

Longing to convey God's love to her own community, she prayerfully considered what her city valued in order to create "touching points" for people to experience God. "I knew that our city would benefit from a story hour for children at our public library, so I asked if we could do this. The city not only wanted us to do this on Saturdays, but asked us to help with events for 500–800 people."[113] For Dedmon, "This is the power of the arts—it is the modern-day 'tongues' in which people can hear God speaking to them in ways that they can understand, which goes beyond language barriers."[114]

Because it is through the inspiration of the Holy Spirit, Dedmon believes all people can be empowered to partner creatively with God, even though some may be more gifted or professionally trained than others.[115] Thus there is an inclusiveness to this ministry, and a call for all people to risk and share in the Spirit's joy of being poured out as God's living water to refresh others. "If we love Jesus, we must be about the Father's business,"

112. Dedmon, *Born to Create*, 164.
113. Ibid., 160.
114. Ibid., 174.
115. Ibid., 138.

and creativity to speak prophetically and in healing ways are "mandated elements of that business."[116]

It is not surprising that one of Dedmon's heroes is Harriet Beecher Stowe, author of *Uncle Tom's Cabin*. She describes the way in which Stowe was faithful in writing articles and stewarding her gift well. This prepared Stowe for the culture-shifting book she would ultimately write, which came to her via "a vision in her church pew of scenes in the book."[117]

Stowe's imaginative, empathetic, and personal style inspired people in ways that treatises, political debates, leaflets, and news accounts could not.[118] Within the first week of publication, *Uncle Tom's Cabin* sold 10,000 copies in the United States, 300,000 in the first year, and in the UK, 1.5 millions copies in one year.[119] Frederick Douglas praised her work saying she had "baptized with holy fire myriads who before cared nothing for the bleeding slave."[120] Though provoking controversy throughout the years for stereotypes she reinforced and her lack of literary "depth and nuance," few people contest *Uncle Tom's Cabin*'s immense impact.[121] Andrew Delbanco claims that *Uncle Tom's Cabin* "helped create or consolidate a reform movement—in Stowe's case, the most consequential reform movement in our history."[122] Ultimately it helped to render unimaginable the exploitation and dehumanization that for a time threatened to split our nation in two.[123]

Stowe attributed the book to God's inspiration, saying, "I did not write it. God wrote it. I merely did his dictation."[124] Stowe wrote in a letter to Lord Denman, "I wrote what I did because as a woman, as a mother I was oppressed and broken-hearted, with the sorrows and injustice I saw, because as a Christian I felt the dishonor to Christianity."[125] Inspiration for

116. Ibid., 222.

117. Ibid.

118. Stowe Center, "Impact of *Uncle Tom's Cabin*, Slavery, and the Civil War."

119. Ibid.

120. Delbanco, "The Impact of 'Uncle Tom's Cabin,'" *The New York Times*, June 26, 2011.

121. Ibid.

122. Ibid.

123. The events surrounding the publication of *Uncle Tom's Cabin* reveal that at times the movement toward reconciliation and healing must face fierce resistance and even endure war, before the ground is level enough to begin to establish relationships of mutuality, justice, and peace.

124. Stowe, Introduction to an 1879 edition of *Uncle Tom's Cabin*.

125. Stowe, "Letter to Lord Denman," January 20, 1853.

this book also arose from years of seeking to know and follow Christ, and from pondering, "How, then, shall a Christian bear fruit?"[126] Her reflections about this in a booklet entitled "How to live on Christ" so impacted Hudson Taylor that in 1869 he sent it to all the missionaries affiliated with the China Inland Mission. Her response to these questions she asked herself was, "There must be a full concentration of the thoughts and affections on Christ; a complete surrender of the whole being to him; a constant looking to him for grace . . . by coming to the Saviour, and making a full, free and hearty surrender of his body, soul and spirit; fully resolved in future to resign the whole to the redeemer's direction."[127] Stowe's holistic commitment to Christ, her openness to the Spirit, and the fruit she was able to bear are a powerful invitation to God's people to join her in drinking more deeply from the wells of God's new creation.[128]

Participation in God's work of new creation calls for deep prayer, reliance on the Holy Spirit, and the empowering vision that the table is set, the wine is poured, and all people are called to come to the feast. May God's people not be like those described by Jesus, who were too preoccupied with other things in their lives to join in the feast, so the host had to send his servants out to the streets and lanes to "bring in the poor, the crippled, the blind, and the lame" with the desire that his "house may be filled" (Luke 14:16–24). May God's people instead receive the vision of God's kingdom, be filled more fully with God's love, and share in the Spirit's purpose to draw all people in. May we live with deep gratitude for God's presence in our midst and the gift of being joined together in Christ with people from every tongue, tribe, and nation, celebrating the new creation.

> Then I saw a new heaven and a new earth; for the first heaven and the first earth had passed away, and the sea was no more. And I saw the holy city, the new Jerusalem, coming down out of heaven from God, prepared as a bride adorned for her husband. And I heard a loud voice from the throne saying, "See, the home of God is among mortals. He will dwell with them; they will be his peoples and God himself will be with them; he will wipe every tear from their eyes. Death will be no more; mourning and crying and pain will be no more, for the first things have passed away . . ." I saw no temple in the city, for its temple is the Lord God the Almighty and

126. Stowe, "Introduction, How to Live on Christ."

127. Ibid.

128. For a description of Stowe's "baptism of the Holy Spirit" see Ruffin, *Profiles in Faith*, 152.

the Lamb. And the city has no need of sun or moon to shine on it, for the glory of God is its light, and its lamp is the Lamb. The nations will walk by its light, and the kings of the earth will bring their glory into it. Its gates will never be shut by day—and there will be no night there. People will bring into it the glory and the honor of the nations. (Rev 21:1–4, 22–26)

Bibliography

Adam, David. *The Cry of the Deer*. London: SPCK/Triangle, 1987.

Athanasius. *Life of Anthony and the Letter to Marcellinus*. Edited by Robert C. Gregg. Mahwah, NJ: Paulist, 1980.

Auden, W. H. *For the Time Being*. Princeton, NJ: Princeton University Press, 2013.

Augustine. *On The Holy Trinity*. In *Nicene and Post-Nicene Fathers*, vol. 3. Translated by Arthur Hadden, edited by Philip Schaff. Edinburgh: T & T Clark, 1998.

Bailyn, Bernard. *Voyagers to the West: A Passage in the Peopling of America on the Eve of the Revolution*. New York: Knopf, 1986.

Bantum, Brian. "Why Christians Can't Be Post-Racial: Christian Existence in the Murky Waters of Race and Place." *The Other Journal* (2009). http://theotherjournal. com/2009/08/17/why-christians-can't-be-post-racial-christian-existence-in-the-murky-waters-of-race-and-place/.

Barfield, Owen. "Either : Or." In *Imagination and the Spirit,* edited by Charles Huttar, 25–42. Grand Rapids: Eerdmans, 1971.

———. "Matter, Imagination, and Spirit." *Journal of American Academy of Religion* 42, no. 4 (1974) 621–29.

Barth, Karl. *The Holy Spirit and the Christian Life: The Theological Basis of Ethics*. Translated by R. Birch Hoyle. Louisville: Westminster John Knox, 1993.

———. "No Christian Marshall Plan." *Christian Century* 65, no. 49, December 8, 1948, 1330–33.

———. "Teach us to Consider." *Interpretation: A Journal of Bible and Theology* 14, no. 2 (1960) 161–66.

———. "A Theological Dialogue." *Theology Today* 19, no. 2 (1962) 171–77.

Bartleman, Frank. *Azusa Street*. Shippensburg, PA: Destiny Image, 2006.

Battle, Michael. *Reconciliation*. Cleveland: Pilgrim, 1997.

Bauckham, Richard, and Trevor Hart. *Hope Against Hope: Christian Eschatology at the Turn of the Millennium*. Grand Rapids: Eerdmans, 1999.

Baum, Gregory. "A Theological Afterword." In *The Reconciliation of Peoples: Challenge to the Churches,* edited by Gregory Baum and Harold Wells, 184–92. Maryknoll, NY: Orbis, 1997.

Benner, David. *The Gift of Being Yourself*. Downers Grove, IL: InterVarsity, 2004.

Bennett, Jill. "The Limits of Empathy and the Global Politics of Belonging." In *Trauma at Home: After 9/11*, edited by Judith Greenberg, 132–38. Lincoln: University of Nebraska Press, 2003.

Berry, Wendell. "Web Exclusive: Wendell Berry Interview Complete Text." Interviewer Rose Marie Berger. *Sojourners*, July, 2004. http://www.sojo.net/index. cfm?action=magazine.article&issue=sojo407&article=040710x

Boesak, Allan Aubrey, and Curtiss Paul DeYoung. *Radical Reconciliation*. Maryknoll, NY: Orbis, 2012.

Bonhoeffer, Dietrich. *Creation and Fall*. Minneapolis: Fortress, 2004.

Boyle, Gregory. *Tattoos on the Heart*. New York: Free Press, 2010.

Bria, Ion. *Go Forth in Peace*. Geneva: WCC, 1986.

Bromiley, G. W. "The Doctrine of Reconciliation: A Survey of Barth's *Kirchliche Dogmatic* IV/2." *The Scottish Journal of Theology* 10 (1957) 76–85.

Brooks, David. "The Humility Code." Seattle Pacific University Downtown Business Breakfast Presentation. April 12, 2012.

———. *Social Animal: The Hidden Sources of Love, Character, and Achievement*. New York: Random House, 2011.

Brown, Brené. *Daring Greatly*. New York: Gotham, 2012.

Brown, Colin, ed. *The New International Dictionary of New Testament Theology*. Grand Rapids: Zondervan, 1971.

Brown, Warren S., Nancey Murphy, and H. Newton Malony, eds. *Whatever Happened to the Soul?* Minneapolis: Fortress, 1998.

Brueggemann, Walter. *Finally Comes the Poet*. Minneapolis: Augsburg Fortress, 1989.

———. *Living Toward the Common Good*. Louisville: Westminster John Knox, 2010.

———. *Living Toward a Vision*. New York: United Church, 1976.

———. *The Practice of the Prophetic Imagination*. Minneapolis: Fortress, 2012.

———. *Spirituality of the Psalms*. Minneapolis: Augsburg Fortress, 2002.

Buber, Martin. *I and Thou*. New York: Scribner, 1958.

Buckley, James J. "A Field of Living Fire: Karl Barth on the Spirit and the Church." *Modern Theology* 10, no. 1 (1994) 81–102.

Byron, William J. "Education, Reconciliation and Social Justice." *Religious Education* 72, no. 3 (1977) 251–61.

Calvin, John. *Institutes of the Christian Religion*, vol. 1. Philadelphia: Westminster, 1960.

Campbell, Douglas. "Reconciliation in Paul: The Gospel of Negation and Transcendence in Galatians 3:28." In *The Theology of Reconciliation*, edited by Colin Gunton, 39–66. London: T & T Clark, 2003.

Castelo, Daniel. "Azusa Street Revival." In *Hispanic-American Religious Cultures*, edited by Miguel De La Torre, 1:424. Santa Barbara, CA: ABC-CLIO, 2009.

———. *Revisioning Pentecostal Ethics—The Epicletic Community*. Cleveland, TN: CPT, 2012.

Cauchi, Tony. "Lucy F. Farrow." In *Revival Library* (2004). http://www.revival-library.org/ pensketches/am_pentecostals/farrow.html.

Cavanaugh, William T. *Torture and Eucharist: Theology, Politics, and the Body of Christ*. Malden, MA: Blackwell, 1998.

Chilcote, Paul Wesley. *Recapturing the Wesleys' Vision*. Downers Grove, IL: InterVarsity Academic, 2004.

Clegg, Cecelia. "Between Embrace and Exclusion." In *Explorations in Reconciliation*, edited by David Tombs and Joseph Liechty, 123–36. Aldershot, UK: Ashgate, 2006.

Coleridge, Samuel Taylor. *Aids to Reflection*. Edited by Henry Nelson Coleridge. Burlington, VT: C. Goodrich, 1840.

———. *Biographia Literaria.* In *Samuel Taylor Coleridge,* edited by H. J. Jackson, 155–482. The Oxford Authors, edited by Frank Kermode. Oxford: Oxford University Press, 1985.

———. "Note to *Confessions.*" In *Confessions of an Inquiring Spirit,* edited by H. St. J. Hart, BD, 81–118. London: William Clowes and Sons, 1853.

Corapi, Wayne. "History and Trinitarian Thought: The Impact of Samuel Taylor Coleridge's Understanding of History on His Conversion to Trinitarian Orthodoxy." MA thesis, Regent College, 1997.

Cox, Harvey. *Fire from Heaven: The Rise of Pentecostal Spirituality and the Reshaping of Religion in the Twenty-First Century.* Reading, MA: Addison-Wesley, 1995.

Crowder, John. *The New Mystics: How to Become Part of the Supernatural Generation.* Shippenberg, PA: Destiny Image, 2006.

Dayton, Donald W. *Toward a Theological Analysis of Pentecostalism.* Metuchen, NJ: Scarecrow, 1987.

De Gruchy, John. *Reconciliation: Restoring Justice.* Minneapolis: Fortress, 2002.

De La Torre, Miguel. *Doing Christian Ethics from the Margins.* Maryknoll, NY: Orbis, 2004.

De Waal, Esther. *The Celtic Vision.* Liguori, MO: Liguori, 1988.

———. *The Celtic Way of Prayer.* New York: Doubleday, 1997.

Dearborn, Kerry. *The Baptized Imagination: The Theology of George MacDonald.* Aldershot, UK: Ashgate, 2006.

———. "The Crucified Christ as the Motherly God: The Theology of Julian of Norwich." *The Scottish Journal of Theology* 55:3 (2002) 283–302.

———. "Recovering a Trinitarian and Sacramental Ecclesiology." In *Evangelical Ecclesiology: Reality or Illusion?,* edited by John G. Stackhouse Jr., 39–73. Grand Rapids: Baker Academic, 2003.

———. "The Sacrament of the Stranger." In *Twentieth-Century Literary Criticism,* edited by Kathy D. Darrow, 297–303. Farmington Hills, MI: Gale, 2012.

Dearborn, Tim. *Beyond Duty: A Passion for Christ, a Heart for Mission.* Seattle: Dynamis Resources, 2013.

Dedmon, Theresa. *Born to Create.* Shippensburg, PA: Destiny Image, 2012.

Dekker, Ted, and Carl Medearis. *Tea with Hezbollah: Sitting at the Enemies' Table, Our Journey through the Middle East.* New York: Doubleday, 2010.

Delbanco, Andrew. "The Impact of 'Uncle Tom's Cabin.'" In *The New York Times,* Sunday Book Review, 18. June 26, 2011.

DeYoung, Curtiss Paul. *Coming Together in the 21st Century.* Valley Forge, PA: Judson, 2009.

Dickerson, Denise. "The African-American Wing of the Wesleyan Tradition." In *The Cambridge Companion to John Wesley,* edited by Randy Maddox et al., 282–97. Cambridge: Cambridge University Press, 2010.

Donne, John. "From 'The Crosse.'" In *The Oxford Book of English Mystical Verse,* edited by D. H. S. Nicholson and A. H. E. Lee, 644. Oxford: Clarendon, 1917.

Doud, Robert E. "The Trinity After Breakfast: Theology and Imagination in Wallace Stevens and Alfred North Whitehead." *Journal of the American Academy of Religion.* 52, no. 2 (1984) 481–98.

Eliot, T. S. "Ash Wednesday." In *The Complete Poems and Plays,* 60–67. New York: Harcourt, Brace & World, 1962.

————. "Four Quartets." In *The Complete Poems and Plays*, 117–45. New York: Harcourt, Brace & World, 1962.

————. "The Waste Land." In *The Complete Poems and Plays*, 37–50. New York: Harcourt, Brace & World, 1962.

Emerson, Michael O., and Christian Smith. *Divided by Faith*. Oxford: Oxford University Press, 2000.

Fee, Gordon. *Listening to the Spirit in the Text*. Grand Rapids: Eerdmans, 2000.

Fimi, Dimitra. "'Mad' Elves and 'Elusive Beauty': Some Celtic Strands of Tolkien's Mythology [1]." *Folklore* 117 (2006) 156–70.

Flowers, Margaret G. "A Wesleyan Theology of Environmental Stewardship." In *"Inward and Outward Health": John Wesley's Holistic Concept of Medical Science, the Environment and Holy Living*, edited by Deborah Madden, 51–93. London: Epworth, 2008.

Fowler, James. "Future Christians and Church Education." In *Hope for the Church: Moltmann in Dialogue with Practical Theology*, edited and translated by Theodore Runyon, 93–111. Nashville: Abingdon, 1979.

Gobodo-Madikizela, Pumla. *A Human Being Died That Night: A South African Woman Confronts the Legacy of Apartheid*. New York: Houghton Mifflin, 2003.

Gopin, Marc. "The Heart of the Stranger." In *Explorations in Reconciliation: New Directions in Theology*, edited by David Tombs and Joseph Liechty, 3–21. Aldershot, UK: Ashgate, 2006.

Gormas, Jan, et al. "Learning as Reconciliation, Learning For Reconciliation: New Dimensions for Christian Secondary Schools." *Journal of Education and Christian Belief* 10, no. 1 (2006) 9–31.

Gouwens, David J. "Kierkegaard on the Ethical Imagination." *Journal of Religious Ethics* 10, no. 2 (1982) 204–20.

Green, Chris E. W. *Toward a Pentecostal Theology of the Lord's Supper*. Cleveland, TN: CPT, 2012.

Green, Garrett. *Imagining God: Theology and the Religious Imagination*. San Francisco: Harper and Row, 1989.

Green, Michael. *Evangelism and the Early Church*. Grand Rapids: Eerdmans, 2003.

The Green Mile. DVD. Directed by Frank Darabont. Los Angeles: Columbia, 2009.

Greenberg, Judith, ed. *Trauma at Home: After 9/11*. Lincoln: University of Nebraska Press, 2003.

Groody, Daniel G. *Globalization, Spirituality, and Justice: Navigating the Path to Peace*. Maryknoll, NY: Orbis, 2007.

Guare, Rita E. "Educating in the Ways of the Spirit: Teaching and Leading Poetically, Prophetically, Powerfully." *Religious Education* 96 (2001) 65–87.

Guroian, Vigen. *Tending the Heart of Virtue: How Classic Stories Awaken a Child's Moral Imagination*. New York: Oxford University Press, 1998.

Gunton, Colin. "Introduction." In *The Theology of Reconciliation*, edited by Colin Gunton, 13–38. London: T & T Clark, 2003.

Gunton, Colin, ed. *The Theology of Reconciliation*. London: T & T Clark, 2003.

Guthrie, Shirley C. *Christian Doctrine*. Louisville: Westminster John Knox, 1994.

Hauerwas, Stanley, et al. *Truthfulness and Tragedy*. Notre Dame: University of Notre Dame Press, 1977.

Hobgood, Mary E. "Flag Waving, Scapegoating, or Solidarity: The Challenge to Whites of the African American Reparations Movement." *Union Seminary Quarterly Review* 56, no. 1–2 (2003) 116–25.

Hollenweger, Walter J. "Towards a Charismatic Theology." In *New Heaven? New Earth?*, edited by Simon Tugwell et al., 9–13. Springfield, IL: Templegate, 1976.

Hughes, Kathleen. "Liturgy and Justice: An Intrinsic Relationship." In *Living No Longer for Ourselves: Liturgy and Justice in the Nineties,* edited by Kathleen Hughes et al., 36–51. Collegeville, MN: Liturgical, 1991.

Hyatt, Eddie L. *2000 Years of Charismatic Christianity*. Lake Mary, FL: Charisma House, 2002.

Irons, Charles. *The Origins of Proslavery Christianity: White and Black Evangelicals in Colonial and Antebellum Virginia*. Chapel Hill, NC: University of North Carolina Press, 2008.

Jackson, John P., and Nadine M. Weidman. "Race and Evolution, 1859–1900." In *Race, Racism and Science: Social Impact and Interaction,* 61–96. New Brunswick, NJ: Rutgers University Press, 2006.

Jennings, Willie James. *The Christian Imagination*. New Haven, CT: Yale University Press, 2010.

Johnson, Andy. "The Sanctification of the Imagination in 1 Thessalonians." In *Holiness and Ecclesiology in the New Testament,* edited by Andy Johnson et al., 275–92. Grand Rapids: Eerdmans, 2007.

Johnson, Jay, et al. "Potential Gains from Trade in Dirty Industries: Revisiting Lawrence Summers' Memo." *Cato Journal* 27, no. 3 (2007) 397–410.

Jones, John Miriam. *With an Eagle's Eye*. Notre Dame, IN: Ave Maria, 1998.

Jones, L. Gregory. *Embodying Forgiveness*. Grand Rapids: Eerdmans, 1995.

Joyce, Timothy J. *Celtic Christianity*. Maryknoll, NY: Orbis, 1998.

Julian of Norwich. *Showings*. Edited by Edmund Colledge and James Walsh. New York: Paulist, 1978.

Jüngel, Eberhard. *God as the Mystery of the World*. Grand Rapids: Eerdmans, 1983.

———. *Theological Essays*. Translated by J. B. Webster. Edinburgh: T & T Clark, 1989.

Kagiwada, Joanne H. "And Justice for All." *Union Seminary Quarterly Review* 56, no. 1–2 (2003) 126–36.

Kärkkäinen, Veli-Matti. "Spirit, Reconciliation and Healing in the Community: Missiological Insights from Pentecostals." *International Review of Mission* 94, no. 372 (2005) 43–50.

———. "Trinity as Communion in the Spirit: Koinonia, Trinity, and Filioque in the Roman Catholic-Pentecostal Dialogue." *Journal of the Society for Pentecostal Studies* 22, no. 2 (2000) 209–30.

Katongole, Emmanuel. *Mirror to the Church*. Grand Rapids: Zondervan, 2009.

———. *The Sacrifice of Africa*. Grand Rapids: Eerdmans, 2011.

Katongole, Emmanuel, and Chris Rice. *Reconciling All Things*. Downers Grove, IL: InterVarsity, 2008.

Kim, Kirsteen. "The Reconciling Spirit: The Dove with Color and Strength." *International Review of Mission* 94, no. 372 (2005) 20–29.

King, Martin Luther, Jr. "Can a Christian Be a Communist?" September 30, 1962. Ebenezer Baptist Church, Atlanta, GA. http://mlk-kppo1.stanford.edu/index.php/encyclopedia/documentsentry/can_a_christian_be_a_communist_30_sept_1962#fn15.

―――. "Where Do We Go From Here?" August 16, 1967. http://mlk-kppo1.stanford. edu/index.php/kingpapers/article/where_do_we_go_from_here/.

Kittel, Gerhard. *Theological Dictionary of the New Testament,* vol. 3. Edited and translated by Geoffrey Bromiley. Grand Rapids: Eerdmans, 1965.

Koyama, Kosuke. *Water Buffalo Theology*. Maryknoll, NY: Orbis, 1999.

Kunz, Sandra. "Imagination and the Discernment of Nonviolent Solutions to Problems of Injustice: Potential Applications of the Work of Christian Educators Paulo Freire, James E. Loder, and Ignatius Loyola to Public Peace Education." *Christian Faith and Violence* 1 (2005) 293–308.

Kurien, Jacob. "Church Unity—Claiming a Common Future." *Ecumenical Review* 58, no. 1 (2006) 118–20.

Kuzmic, Peter. "Reconciliation in Eastern Europe." In *Reconciliation in Difficult Places: Dealing with Our Deepest Differences*, edited by the Office of Advocacy and Education, 46–55. Monrovia, CA: World Vision, 1994.

LaCugna, Catherine Mowry. *God for Us: The Trinity and Christian Life*. New York: HarperCollins, 1991.

Laub, Dori. "Truth and Testimony." *American Imago* 48 (1991) 85.

Lederach, John Paul. *The Moral Imagination: The Art and Soul of Building Peace*. Oxford: Oxford University Press, 2004.

Levison, Jack R. *Filled with the Spirit*. Grand Rapids: Eerdmans, 2009.

Lewis, C. S. *George MacDonald: An Anthology*. London: G. Bles, 1946.

―――. *The Great Divorce*. New York: HarperCollins, 2001.

―――. *The Last Battle*. New York: HarperCollins, 1984.

―――. "Letter to Sister Penelope." In *The Collected Letters of C. S. Lewis*, edited by Walter Hooper, 2:262. San Francisco: HarperSanFrancisco, 2004.

Liardon, Roberts. *Azusa Street Revival*. Shippensburg, PA: Destiny Image, 2006.

―――. *God's Generals: The Revivalists*. Sarasota, FL: Whitaker House, 2008.

Liechty, Joseph. "Putting Forgiveness in its Place: The Dynamics of Reconciliation." In *Explorations in Reconciliation*, edited by David Tombs et al., 59–68. Aldershot, UK: Ashgate, 2006.

Luther, Martin. *Heidelberg Disputation*. 1518. *Luther's Works,* vol. 1. Edited by Harold J. Grimm. Philadelphia: Muhlenburg, 1957.

―――. *Operationes in Psalmos*. In *The Pastoral Luther: Essays on Martin Luther's Practical Theology,* edited by Timothy J. Wengert, 33–56. Lutheran Quarterly Books, edited by Paul Rorem et al. Grand Rapids, Eerdmans, 2009.

MacDonald, George. *The Golden Key and Other Fantasy Stories*. Grand Rapids: Eerdmans, 1980.

―――. "The Imagination." In *Dish of Orts*, 1–42. Whitehorn, CA: Johannesen, 1996.

―――. *Phantastes*. Tring, UK: Lion, 1982.

Machado, Daisy L. "The Historical Imagination and Latina/o Rights." *Union Seminary Quarterly Review* 56, no. 1–2 (2003) 155–68.

Mackey, James P., ed. *An Introduction to Celtic Christianity*. Edinburgh: T & T Clark, 1995.

Madden, Deborah. "Introduction: Saving Souls and Saving Lives." In *"Inward and Outward Health": John Wesley's Holistic Concept of Medical Science, the Environment and Holy Living,* edited by Deborah Madden, 1–14. London: Epworth, 2008.

Maddox, Randy. "'Honoring Conference': Wesleyan Reflections on the Dynamics of Theological Reflection." *Methodist Review* 4 (2012) 77–116.

————. "John Wesley on Holistic Health and Healing." *Methodist History* 46, no. 1 (2007) 4–33.

————. "Reclaiming the Eccentric Parent." In *"Inward and Outward Health": John Wesley's Holistic Concept of Medical Science, the Environment and Holy Living*, edited by Deborah Madden, 15–50. London: Epworth, 2008.

Marquardt, Manfred. *John Wesley's Social Ethics*. Nashville: Abingdon, 1992.

Marsh, Charles, and John Perkins. *Welcoming Justice*. Downers Grove, IL: InterVarsity, 2009.

Martin, Larry. *The Life and Ministry of William J. Seymour*. Joplin, MO: Christian Life, 1999.

Matar, Hisham. "Hisham Matar on the Power of Libyan Fiction." National Public Radio, April 28, 2011. http://www.npr.org/2011/04/28/135782783/hisham-matar-on-the-power-of-libyan-fiction.

McClung, Grant. *Azusa Street and Beyond*. South Plainsfield, NJ: Bridge, 1986.

McIntyre, John. *Faith Theology and Imagination*. Edinburgh: Handsel, 1987.

————. *The Shape of Pneumatology*. Edinburgh, T & T Clark, 1997.

Moltmann. Jürgen. *The Coming of God*. Minneapolis: Fortress, 1996.

————. *The Source of Life*. Translated by Margaret Kohl. London: SCM, 1997.

————. *The Spirit of Life: A Universal Affirmation*. Translated by Margaret Kohl. Minneapolis: Fortress, 2001.

————. *Theology of Hope*. Minneapolis: Fortress, 1993.

Morrison, Toni. *Playing in the Dark*. Cambridge, MA: Harvard University Press, 1992.

Moucarry, Chawkat. *The Search for Forgiveness*. Leicester, UK: InterVarsity, 2004.

Musalaha staff letter. June 17, 2010. http://www.musalaha.org.

Nalunnakkal, George Matthew. "Come Holy Spirit, Heal and Reconcile: Called in Christ to Be Reconciling and Healing Communities." *International Review of Mission* 94, no. 372 (2005) 7–19.

Niles, Preman. "Costly Grace: Race and Reconciliation—An Asian Perspective." *Union Seminary Quarterly Review* 56, no. 1–2 (2003) 147–53.

Nouwen, Henri J. M. *A Letter of Consolation*. San Francisco: Harper & Row, 1982.

————. *Road to Peace*. Edited by John Dear. Maryknoll, NY: Orbis, 1998.

————. *Sabbatical Journey: The Diary of His Final Year*. New York: Crossroad, 1998.

Ó Ríordáin, John J. *The Music of What Happens*. Winona, MN: St. Mary's, 1996.

Perkins, John. "Contexts of the Journey of Reconciliation." Presentation for Duke Center for Reconciliation Summer Institute: "Shaping the Beloved Community." Durham, NC, June 1, 2009.

————. *Let Justice Roll Down*. Ventura, CA: Regal, 1976.

Pew Research Forum. "Pentecostal Resource Page." October 5, 2006. http://www.pewforum.org/Christian/Evangelical-Protestant-Churches/Pentecostal-Resource-Page.aspx.

Pierson, Paul. *Dynamics of Christian Mission: History through a Missiological Perspective*. Pasadena, CA: William Carey, 2009.

Pinnock, Clark. *Flame of Love*. Downers Grove, IL: InterVarsity, 1996.

Prickett, Stephen. *Victorian Fantasy*. Brighton: Harvester, 1979.

Rah, Soong-Chan. *The Next Evangelicalism*. Downers Grove, IL: InterVarsity, 2009.

Rigg, James H. *The Living Wesley*. London: Charles H. Kelley, 1981.

Rohr, Richard. *Falling Upward: A Spirituality for the Two Halves of Life*. San Francisco: Jossey-Bass, 2011.

Ruffin, C. Bernard. *Profiles in Faith*. Liguori, MO: Liguori/Triumph, 1997.

Salter-McNeil, Brenda. *A Credible Witness*. Downers Grove, IL: InterVarsity, 2008.

———. *The Heart of Racial Justice*. Downers Grove, IL: InterVarsity, 2004.

Satyavrata, Ivan. *The Holy Spirit, Lord and Life-Giver*. Downers Grove, IL: InterVarsity, 2009.

Schreiter, Robert J. *The Ministry of Reconciliation*. Maryknoll, NY: Orbis, 1998.

Schwöbel, Christoph. "Reconciliation: From Biblical Observations to Dogmatic Reconstruction." In *The Theology of Reconciliation*, edited by Colin Gunton, 13–38. London: T & T Clark, 2003.

Sellner, Edward C. *Wisdom of the Celtic Saints*. Notre Dame, IN: Ave Maria, 1993.

Sider, Ronald J. *The Scandal of the Evangelical Conscience: Why Are Christians Living Just Like the Rest of the World?* Grand Rapids: Baker, 2005.

Smith, Gordon. *The Voice of Jesus*. Downers Grove, IL: InterVarsity, 2003.

Smith, James K. A. *Thinking in Tongues: Pentecostal Contributions to Christian Philosophy*. Grand Rapids, Eerdmans, 2010.

Snyder, Graydon. *Irish Jesus, Roman Jesus*. Harrisburg, PA: Trinity, 2002.

Snyder, Howard. *The Radical Wesley*. Downers Grove, IL: InterVarsity, 1980.

Snyder, Howard, and Joel Scandrett. *Salvation Means Creation Healed*. Eugene, OR: Cascade, 2011.

Song, C. S. "Telling Stories of the Spirit's Movement in Asia." In *Doing Theology with the Spirit's Movement in Asia*, edited by John England and Alan Torrance, 1–14. Singapore: ATSEA, 1991.

Stiglitz, Joseph. *The Price of Inequality*. New York: Norton, 2012.

Stowe Center. "Impact of *Uncle Tom's Cabin*, Slavery, and the Civil War." http://www.harrietbeecherstowecenter.org/utc/impact.shtml

Stowe, Harriet Beecher. "Letter to Lord Denman" (January 20, 1853). In *Harriet Beecher Stowe: A Life*, by Joan D. Hedrick. New York: Oxford University Press, 1994.

———. "Introduction, How to Live on Christ." In *Religion as It Should Be*, by Christopher C. Dean. Boston: Massachusetts Sabbath School Society, 1847. http://www.path2prayer.com/article/579/victory-overcoming-temptation/harriet-beecher-stowe-how-to-live-on-christ

———. *Uncle Tom's Cabin*. Boston: Houghton, Mifflin, 1879.

Strengel, Richard. *Mandela's Way*. New York: Crown, 2009.

Synan, Vinson. *The Holiness-Pentecostal Tradition: Charismatic Movements in the Twentieth Century*. Grand Rapids: Eerdmans, 1977.

———. "The Origins of the Pentecostal Movement." http://www.oru.edu/library/special_collections/holy_spirit_research_center/pentecostal_history.php.

Thompson, Curtis L. "Interpreting God's Translucent World." In *Translucence: Religion, the Arts, and Imagination*, edited by Carol Gilbertson et al., 3–37. Minneapolis: Fortress, 2004.

Thompson-Cannino, Jennifer, and Ronald Cotton. *Picking Cotton*. New York: St. Martin's, 2009.

Tillard, J. M. R. "Spirit, Reconciliation, Church." *Ecumenical Review* 42, no. 3–4 (1990) 237–49.

Tolkien, J. R. R. *The Silmarillion*. New York: Ballantine, 2002.

Tomkins, Stephen. *John Wesley: A Biography*. Grand Rapids: Eerdmans, 2003.

Torrance, Alan. "Accounts of the Spirit's Movement in Aotearoa/New Zealand: An Ethical and Theological Dilemma." In *Doing Theology with the Spirit's Movement in Asia*, edited by John C. England et al., 62–84. Singapore: ATSEA, 1991.

———. "The Theological Grounds for Advocating Forgiveness." In *The Politics of Past Evil: Religion, Reconciliation and the Dilemmas of Transitional Justice*, edited by Daniel Philpott, 45–80. Notre Dame, IN: University of Notre Dame Press, 2006.

Torrance, James. *Worship, Community and the Triune God of Grace*. Downers Grove, IL: InterVarsity, 1996.

Torrance, T. F. *Theology in Reconstruction*. London: SCM, 1965.

Tugwell, Simon. "The Speech-Giving Spirit: A Dialogue with Tongues." In *New Heaven? New Earth?*, edited by Simon Tugwell et al., 119–59. Springfield, IL: Templegate, 1976.

Turner, Max. "Human Reconciliation in the New Testament with Special Reference to Philemon, Colossians and Ephesians." *European Journal of Theology* 16, no. 1 (2006) 37–47.

Tutu, Desmond. "BBC Breakfast with Frost." May 29, 2005. http://news.bbc.co.uk/2/hi/programmes/breakfast_with_frost/4591113.stm.

———. *Made for Goodness: And Why This Makes All the Difference*. New York: HarperCollins, 2011.

———. "My Search for God." St. Mary's Jubilee Lenten Talks, St. Alban's, Ferreirarstown, April 5, 1979.

Van Kooten, George. "The 'Church of God' and Civic Assemblies of the Greek Cities in the Roman Empire: A Response to Paul Trebilco and Richard Horsley." *New Testament Studies* 58, no. 4 (2012) 522–48.

Van Slyke, Daniel G. "The Changing Meanings of *sacramentum*: Historical Sketches." *Antiphon* 11, no. 3 (2007) 245–79.

Vassiliadis, Petros. "Reconciliation as a Pneumatalogical Mission Paradigm: Some Preliminary Reflections by an Orthodox." *International Review of Mission* 94, no. 372 (2005) 30–42.

Verwoerd, Wilhelm. "Toward Inclusive Remembrance after the 'Troubles': A Philosophical Perspective from within the South African Truth and Reconciliation Commission." In *Explorations in Reconciliation*, edited by David Tombs et al., 103–22. Aldershot, UK: Ashgate, 2006.

Volf, Miroslav. *Exclusion and Embrace*. Nashville: Abingdon, 1996.

———. "A Theology of Embrace for a World of Exclusion." In *Explorations in Theology: New Directions in Theology*, edited by David Tombs et al., 22–33. Aldershot, UK: Ashgate, 2006.

Von Balthasar, Hans Urs. *The Glory of the Lord: A Theological Aesthetics*, vol. 1. New York: Crossroad, 1982.

Wagner, C. Peter. "Characteristics of Pentecostal Church Growth." In *Azusa Street and Beyond*, edited by Grant McClung, 127–30. South Plainsfield, NJ: Bridge, 1986.

Wall, Rob. "Waiting on the Holy Spirit." *Journal of Pentecostal Theology* 22 (2013) 37–53.

Wan, Sze-kar. *Power in Weakness: Conflict and Rhetoric in Paul's Second Letter to the Corinthians*. Harrisburg, PA: Trinity, 2000.

Wangerin, Walt. "The Ragman." In *Ragman and Other Cries of Faith*, 3–6. San Francisco: Harper & Row, 1984.

Ware, Kallistos. *The Orthodox Way*. Crestwood, NY: St. Vladimir's Seminary Press, 1976.

Watts, Rikk E. "The New Exodus/New Creational Restoration of the Image of God." In *What Does It Mean to Be Saved?*, edited by John G. Stackhouse Jr., 15–41. Grand Rapids: Baker Academic, 2002.

Wesley, John. *Explanatory Notes Upon the New Testament*. London: Epworth, 1966.

———. "The General Deliverance." Sermon 60. In *The Works of John Wesley*, edited by Albert C. Outler, 2:437–50. Nashville: Abingdon, 1985.

———. "The Good Steward." Sermon 51. In *The Works of John Wesley*, edited by Albert C. Outler, 2:281–98. Nashville: Abingdon, 1985.

———. *Journal*, Jan. 1, 1739. In *The Works of John Wesley, Volume 19: Journal and Diaries II (1738-43)*, edited by W. Reginald Ward (Journal) and Richard P. Heitzenrater (Diaries), *The Bicentennial Edition of the Works of John Wesley*, edited by Richard P. Heitzenrater and Frank Baker, 29. Nashville: Abingdon, 1990.

———. *Journal*, April 2, 1739. In *The Works of John Wesley, Volume 19: Journal and Diaries II (1738-43)*, edited by W. Reginald Ward (Journal) and Richard P. Heitzenrater (Diaries), *The Bicentennial Edition of the Works of John Wesley*, edited by Richard P. Heitzenrater and Frank Baker, 46. Nashville: Abingdon, 1990.

———. *Journal*, October 12, 1739. In *The Works of John Wesley, Volume 19: Journal and Diaries II (1738-43)*, edited by W. Reginald Ward (Journal) and Richard P. Heitzenrater (Diaries), *The Bicentennial Edition of the Works of John Wesley*, edited by Richard P. Heitzenrater and Frank Baker, 104-105. Nashville: Abingdon, 1990.

———. *Journal*, August 15, 1750. In *The Works of John Wesley, Volume 20: Journal and Diaries III (1743-1754)*, edited by W. Reginald Ward (Journal) and Richard P. Heitzenrater (Diaries), *The Bicentennial Edition of the Works of John Wesley*, edited by Richard P. Heitzenrater and Frank Baker, 356-357. Nashville: Abingdon, 1991.

———. "Letter to Wilberforce," In *The Works of John Wesley*, edited by Thomas Jackson, 13:153. 1872. Grand Rapids: Zondervan, 1958.

———. "The More Excellent Way," Sermon 89, §2. In *The Works of John Wesley*, edited by Albert C. Outler, 3:263–64. Nashville: Abingdon, 1985.

———. "The New Creation." Sermon 64. In *The Works of John Wesley*, edited by Albert C. Outler, 2:500–510. Nashville: Abingdon, 1985.

———. "On Visiting the Sick." Sermon 98. In *The Works of John Wesley*, edited by Albert C. Outler, 3:384–97. Nashville: Abingdon, 1985.

———. *A Plain Account of Christian Perfection*, §2. In *The Works of John Wesley*, vol. 13, edited by Richard P. Heitzenrater, Randy L. Maddox, and Frank Baker, 136–91. Nashville: Abingdon, 2013.

———. *The Principles of a Methodist, further explained*, IV.1. In *The Works of John Wesley*, edited by Albert C. Outler, 9:211. Nashville: Abingdon, 1985.

———. *Thoughts upon Slavery*. In *The Works of John Wesley*, edited by Thomas Jackson, 11:59–79. Grand Rapids: Zondervan, 1958.

Willard, Dallas. *Divine Conspiracy*. San Francisco: HarperSanFrancisco, 1998.

Williams, Rowan. *On Christian Theology*. Oxford: Blackwell, 2000.

Williston, Walker. *A History of the Christian Church*. New York: Scribner, 1918.

Wirzba, Norman, *Living the Sabbath: Discovering the Rhythms of Rest and Delight*. Grand Rapids: Brazos, 2006.

Wolff, Hans Walter. *Dodekapropheton 2: Joel und Amos*. Neukirchen: Verlag der Buchhandlung des Erziehungsverein, 1956.

Wright, Christopher J. H. *Knowing the Holy Spirit through the Old Testament*. Downers Grove, IL: InterVarsity Academic, 2006.

Wright, N. T. *How God Became King*. New York: HarperCollins, 2011.

Yong, Amos. *Who Is the Holy Spirit?* Brewster, MA: Paraclete, 2011.

Zurara, Gomes Eannes De. *The Chronicle of the Discovery and Conquest of Guinea*. Vol 1. New York: Burt Franklin, 1963.